CLASSIC

SAVANNAH

History, Homes, and Gardens

CLASSIC
SAVANNAH

History, Homes, and Gardens

PHOTOGRAPHY BY VAN JONES MARTIN
TEXT BY WILLIAM ROBERT MITCHELL, JR.

MARTIN~St. MARTIN PUBLISHING COMPANY
NEW ORLEANS • SAVANNAH
A GOLDEN COAST BOOK

DEDICATION

To James Edward Oglethorpe
and all who have helped
build, preserve, and restore Savannah.

Third Printing.

ISBN 0-932958-07-9, clothbound.

Library of Congress
Card Catalog No. 87-80408

Copyright © 1991 by
Golden Coast Publishing Company,
22 Waite Drive, Savannah, Georgia 31406
Telephone (912)352-1809

Designed and produced by Lisa Lytton-Smith.

Copyedited by Kathleen Bergen Durham.

Color separations by Savannah Color
Separations, Inc.

Printed in Hong Kong by Everbest Printing
Co., Ltd., through Four Colour Imports, Ltd.,
Louisville, Kentucky.

Special thanks to Hansell (Hank) Ramsey for
the use of the photograph on page ten.

HALF-TITLE LOGO	Detail, Trustees' View, 1734, cottages and garden parterres on town lots, Derby Ward.
FRONTISPIECE	William Scarbrough House, 1819, 41 West Broad Street, Oglethorpe Ward.
TITLE PAGE	Walled garden, William Battersby House, 1852, 119 East Charlton Street, Lafayette Square.
CONTENTS PAGE	James Habersham, Jr., House, "Old Pink House," 23 Abercorn Street, Reynolds Square.

Acknowledgments

For each of those who helped either Van or me, the most eloquent thank you I can make is the book itself. *Classic Savannah*, in overall form and detail, and on every page, acknowledges the help of gracious, generous, and talented people. These are only some of those whose interest or help deserves special recognition: Maryellen Higgenbotham and the staff of the Isaiah Davenport House; Executive Director Neil Horstman and Dee McCoy of Historic Savannah Foundation; Dolly Tyson and the staff of the Owens-Thomas House; Feay Shellman Coleman, Harry DeLorme, and Elizabeth Scott Shatto of the Telfair Academy of Arts and Sciences; Fran Powell, Joanne Newbery, Stephen Bohlin-Davis, and Katherine Keena, and the staff of the Juliette Gordon Low Center; Mrs. Bernard Williams and the staff of the Andrew Low House; the St. John's Episcopal Church; Colonel William E. Harper, Jr.; the staff of the reference desk at the main branch of the Savannah Public Library; Barbara Bennett, Tracy Bearden, and the staff of the Georgia Historical Society; David Kaminsky, Rusty Smith, Bob Holladay, and Sarah Sowell at Savannah Color Separations; Emma and Lee Adler; Mrs. E. J. Benton, Jr.; David Byers; Mrs. John Wright Carswell, Sr.; Lois Crossley; Mr. and Mrs. Mitchell Dunn; Mr. and Mrs. Wiley Ellis; Kenneth Garcia; Don and Pat Harper; Mrs. Walter C. (Connie) Hartridge II; George and Katrin Haskell; Mr. and Mrs. Ed Hill; Mr. and Mrs. Ira Koger; Mills Lane IV; John LeBey; Dr. and Mrs. Alston McCaslin; Francis McNairy; Sam Mangham; Joseph Moore; Mary Morrison; James Morton; Alvin Neely; Mrs. Harry Norman; Dr. and Mrs. Lamont Osteen; Dean Owens; Hank and Jean Ramsey; John and Beth Reiter; Ed and Esther Shaver; Bryan Shrum; Arthur Smith; Bess Stanley; Albert Stoddard; Kenneth Thomas; Frank Walsh; Jim Williams; Louisa Wood; Mr. and Mrs. David A. Young; Van's wife, Barbara; and my mother, Miriam Mitchell.

William R. Mitchell, Jr.
Georgia Day, 12 February, 1987

I was born in the old Telfair Hospital at the foot of Forsyth Park, because at that time the nearest hospital to Riceboro was in Savannah. Dr. Ruskin King was my pediatrician, and Dr. John Kirk Train prescribed my first pair of glasses when I was in the third grade. Even after we moved to St. Simons we still made the hazardous journey up U.S. 17 to our various doctors. "Coming to town" was a big deal then—a sweater and slacks and my best shoes, breakfast on the porch of the DeSoto, a doctor's appointment, a stop at the Hobby Shop, and a milkshake at the Howard Johnson's on 17 on the way home. Mama didn't shop for herself on those trips—she came up alone and got a room at the DeSoto when she wanted to spend some serious time at Fine's and the Globe.

I thought little of Savannah after I stopped coming up to the doctor, but when I began photographing historic architecture my travels naturally led me back. One day, while documenting the houses on West Taylor Street for the book *Historic Savannah*, I shuddered with the realization that the beautiful old dutch-gabled house I was trying to photograph was the scene of countless anxious hours spent waiting to have blood squeezed from the tip of my finger. I had never even seen the gable of that house before, my focus was so fixed on the side stair and the iron railing that led to Dr. King's waiting room and torture chamber.

From that moment, I perceived Savannah and, for that matter, all architecture, differently. I began to feel the continuum of time and human experiences in each building I photographed. If my piddling visits to a pediatrician could so transform this stucco house in my mind, the public pageants of historic events and the private dramas of individual lives spinning through Savannah for two and one-half centuries must have marked in some way each house, each ballast stone wall, each mantelpiece and handrail in the city.

This imprint, usually obvious but often subtle, is seldom more palpable than that of a family on its home. In *Classic Savannah*, we have tried to present this evidence, from the reconstructed interiors of museum houses to the homes of contemporary Savannahians, with examples of the houses we have built and the homes in which we live. Beyond the museum houses, there is probably little consensus on which houses should have been chosen for such a book. Our selections were made using the following criteria: quality of design and craftsmanship; diversity of style and building materials; historical importance; and neighborhood representation.

By comparing early "prospects" and subsequent "bird's-eye" views, Bill Mitchell has described and analyzed the evolution of one of the most remarkable cities in America. Savannah has experienced tremendous changes in scale, pace, fashion, size, and custom, but I am often struck by the continuity of the old place. The low light of autumn crawls its same October paths across parlor floors, spotlighting furniture and accoutrements as it did in 1779, when my great-great-great-grandfather was felled by cannon shot at the Spring Hill redoubt; the early morning north summer light that licks the faces of the tall rows on River Street is the same as that my youthful grandfather saw when he worked the docks as a night watchman; and the color filtering through the new live oak leaves in the squares will be the same this spring as it was when I came to town as a child, so completely ignorant of the enduring charm and beauty of Savannah.

Van Jones Martin
February 8, 1987

Van Martin and I listed ourselves alphabetically in the first book we did together, *Landmark Homes of Georgia, 1733–1983*. My "i" still followed Martin's alphabetical "a" in our second book, *The Architecture of William Frank McCall, Jr., FAIA*, and does so in this, our third collaboration. As before, both of us had primary duties while serving as co-editors. His first responsibility was photography and mine was history and words, or what is usually called text.

My dictionary defines text as "the original written or printed words and form of an original work." In truth, both of us have given form to our books. As dual editors, we collaborate smoothly. Friction, if at all, comes only from a useful exchange of ideas. Our intention is to mold a harmonious unity from my history and his photography. In this, a third person has very important work, Lisa Lytton-Smith, whose title would be graphic designer or possibly art director, if those who collaborate under the corporate mantle of Golden Coast Publishing Company actually used titles.

I do not live in Savannah, but in the city of Atlanta where I was born. Yet I did much of the research, writing, and other work while I was the guest of my mother in her restored row house in the Savannah Historic District, as I had during the preparation of *Landmark Homes of Georgia*.

My very first visit to Savannah was in 1939 before I was a year old. Documentation of this (historians are compelled) is a snapshot. I am a baby being cradled by my father at Savannah Beach on Tybee Island, where my parents were guests at the Amfico Club of the Atlantic Mutual Fire Insurance Company. Since that babe-in-arms visit, I have returned to Savannah often, especially after my mother restored a Historic District house as a project that became permanent residence. Her genealogical research, after moving to Savannah to live, even documented an ancestral association with the town; one of her, and thus one of my, eighteenth-century forebears resided on the northwest trust lot of Johnson Square in a house that was destroyed in the fire of 1796.

My suggestion of the title *Classic Savannah* was derived from a long-held conviction that Savannah is historic, yes, but more. Classic, the dictionary defines in this way: "Of recognized value; serving as a standard of excellence; historically memorable; noted because of special historical associations; authentic." And Savannah is all of that.

The appealing landscaped geometry of downtown squares surrounded by architecture-rich wards developed sequentially from the 1730s through the 1850s, and then preserved and restored in the twentieth century, is a charmingly unique *urbs*. It is a place that truly meets the definition of classicism: "Adherence to traditional and enduringly valid standards, as of simplicity, restraint, and proportion." The simplicity, restraint, and proportion of Savannah, Georgia, is indeed an enduringly valid standard of excellence. It is this that Van Martin and I sought to capture in our book.

William R. Mitchell, Jr.
Georgia Day, 12 February, 1987

CONTENTS

Georgian Savannah, Georgia

SAVANNAH IS A GEORGIAN CITY in ways even more fundamental than its location within the boundaries of Georgia. Georgian England produced Savannah—a formative influence that continued long after the American Revolution. Modified by the southern latitude of Savannah and the passage of time, the style of eighteenth- and early nineteenth-century Georgian England is the primary heritage of Savannah.

Founded during the reign of the namesake of the colony, George II, Savannah grew increasingly Georgian under George III, when the town became the seat of government in 1752 for the newly proclaimed Royal Colony. The royal governors brought prosperity unknown during James Edward Oglethorpe's utopian yet militarily successful Trusteeship. Even after the Revolution, when the English colony became an American state and the state capital was removed inland, Savannah maintained strong cultural, social, and mercantile ties with George IV's regency and reign. A prime example of this is the Regency architecture of William Jay, a talented young English architect who came to Savannah in 1817 and built landmarks of neoclassicism that still grace the squares of Savannah.

After George III's granddaughter Victoria succeeded to the throne in 1837, the ties Savannah had with England strengthened even more. When Victoria became queen, cotton was king, and the Georgian atmosphere of squares and row houses in Savannah constantly got fresh inspiration from across and along the Atlantic. Ideas about architecture, interiors, and gardens arrived directly from England and were adapted to suit Savannah. From ports along the eastern seaboard as far north as New England came the additional influence of other American adaptations of Georgian taste, giving piquancy to the fundamentally British character of Savannah. In a brilliant essay, the late Savannah historian, Walter Charlton Hartridge, wrote about the antebellum affinity of Savannah for England: "The British Consul in Savannah enjoyed more prestige than any Royal Governor of Colonial days. The Cotton Exchange at Liverpool became the magnet which held the aspirations of the town" (1947, p. 4).

Named for the tidal river on which Oglethorpe and the Trustees of Georgia located the original settlement in 1733, Savannah changed slowly until its English "Georgianness" became an entrenched tradition. Many contend Savannah cherishes this Georgian heritage more than its status as a city and county seat within the state whose "geographical surname" it bears. (For Savannah, it is the other way around—Savannah gave Georgia its legitimate birth.)

This tradition of Georgian Savannah, Georgia, was noted by the great English historian J. H. Plumb. Writing at the time of the American Bicentennial, Plumb commented: "The impress of Georgian England, the most beautiful age of British architecture and art, goes as deep in Savannah as it does in Bath . . . or in the great Georgian terraces of Edinburgh" (1976, p. 15).

The first, richest, and busiest seaport in Georgia—and in 1986 ranked twelfth in the United States—Savannah is the cynosure of old, low-country Georgia, of the antebellum past of the state, and of the era "after the War" when a busy trade in cotton, phosphates, timber, and naval stores made the port rich again. From that post–Civil War prosperity came superb buildings that followed the latest Victorian fashions in architecture but with a subdued, late-Georgian reserve that suited the conservative taste of Savannah.

Savannah, the county seat of Chatham, is sometimes called the kingdom of Chatham because of its royal Georgian background and because, too, of its world importance when the present capital of Georgia—Atlanta, founded in 1837 and declared the capital in 1868—was a railroad terminus in the red clay hills of north Georgia. As a kingdom unto itself, Savannah and its well-shod "silk-stockinged" feet are firmly placed on the sandy soil where Oglethorpe blocked off the first four squares of His Majesty's embryo English town in 1733.

By 1851, the number of these four squares had multiplied to twenty-four, forming the primary feature of the unique town plan, Georgian in character, that was recognized in 1966 as the largest National Historic Landmark District in the United States. Over time, Savannah has evolved into a classic city, now recognized throughout the world for its historic beauty and civilized pace in our out-of-breath century.

Classic Savannah is about living in this city where heritage and charm are civic virtues; where the power of the past is not denied but relished and proclaimed; where Georgian means British origins, styles and fashions, character, atmosphere, and affinities modified by the deep southern latitude of Savannah.

Welcome, ladies and gentlemen, and make yourselves at home in Savannah, Georgia, a twentieth-century Georgian town.

William R. Mitchell, Jr.
October 1986

The Reverend Charles Rogers House, 1858, 425 Bull Street, Monterey Square.

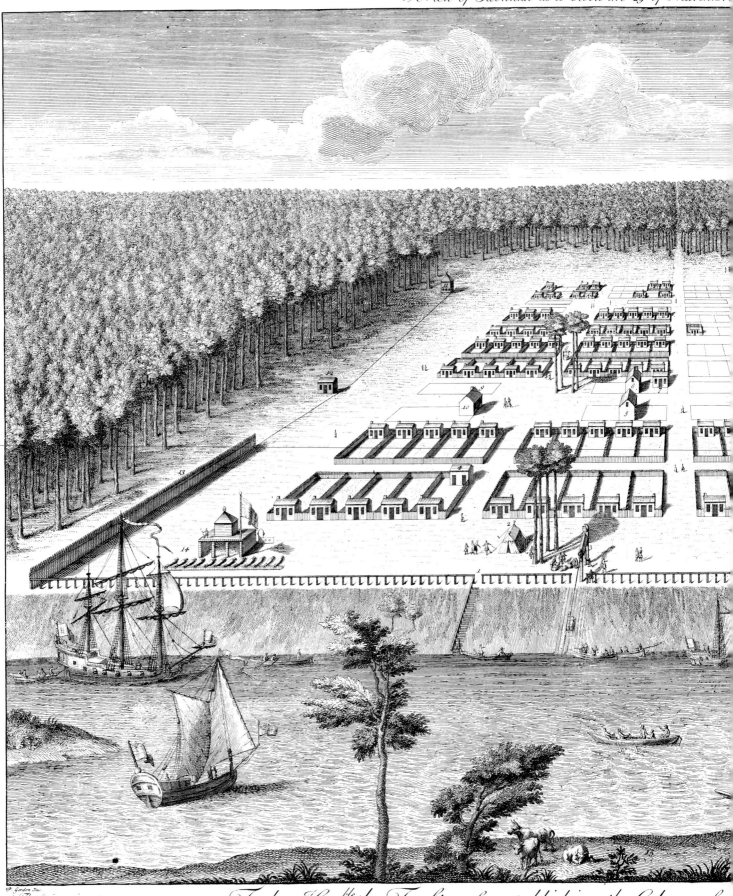

P. Gordon Inv.

1. *The Stairs going up.*
2. *Mr. Oglethorpe's Tent.*
3. *The Crane & Bell.*
4. *The Tabernacle & Court House.*
5. *The publick Mill.*
6. *The House for Strangers.*
7. *The publick Oven.*
8. *The draw Well.*

To the Hon.ᵇˡᵉ the Trustees for establishing the Colony of G...

This View of the Town of Savanah is humbly dedicated by t...

Obliged...

12

ia in America

Honours

st Obedient Servant

Peter Gordon

9. The Lott for the Church.
10. The publick Stores.
11. The Fort.
12. The Parsonage house.
13. The Pallisadoes.
14. The Guard house and Battery of Cannon.
15. Hatchinsons Island.

P. Fourdrinier Sculp.

Oglethorpe-Gordon-Fourdrinier View of Savannah, 1734. This elegant bird's-eye prospect shows the town as it stood when Oglethorpe left for England after his first year in the colony. It was engraved in London in the summer of 1734 by a master engraver whose work Oglethorpe knew well (P. Fourdrinier, Sculp.). For the Georgia Trustees, Peter Gordon handled details of having the view drawn, engraved, and printed (P. Gordon, Inv.). This was the first view the world had of a unique interpretation of English Georgian town planning—a fortified series of London squares—for Oglethorpe's philanthropic, mercantile, and military undertaking in America. His tent (number 2) is near the center of the print in the area that is now a park along Bay Street. Just to the right is Bull Street as it enters Johnson Square, Derby Ward—the first of the units consisting of a central square, a surrounding ward of identical frame cottages, and trust lots for public buildings (numbers 5, 6, 9 and 10) which Oglethorpe laid out in 1733. Johnson Square and Bull Street became the center of the original town as it grew from the four units shown here, to six in 1743 when Oglethorpe left Georgia to return to England permanently. By the 1850s, there were twenty-four, all of which in 1966 were declared a 2.2-square-mile National Historic Landmark District.

INTRODUCTION

"Resolve'd to establish . . . a Town on the River Savannah
to be call'd by that name. 1 Novbr. 1732."

The Journal of the Earl of Egmont
"Abstract of the Trustees Proceedings, 1732–1738."

LONDON FIRST GLIMPSED SAVANNAH in an engraved bird's-eye view—
"Savanah as it stood the 29th of March 1734"; the new settlement on the
southern frontier of His Majesty's American colonies was so far removed
and unfamiliar that its name was misspelled. Nevertheless, the view
showed a well-ordered colonial outpost, with the outlines of an extraordinary town plan—a proposed series of wards organized as an assemblage of
residential squares similar to those being developed singly in London. Behind the beginnings of a palisade was the embryo of an English town in a
sandy clearing almost entirely surrounded by tall pines.

In George II's England this kind of view, called a prospect, was ex-
tremely popular. A phrase used at the time told a great deal: "gilded scenes
and shining prospects." The first, most historic prospect of Savannah elegantly depicted a dreamlike, colonial Georgian town that could promise
little but the "shining prospects" of some future time. "Dedicated to the
Trustees for establishing the Colony of Georgia in America," it showed

Bay Street divided by Bull Street, sketched in
1786 by Major Edward White, a Savannah
Custom House officer. *Georgia Historical Society.*

Savannah a bit more than a year after James Edward Oglethorpe, the only Trustee to go to the colony, first pitched his tent and settled a needy band of colonists on Yamacraw Bluff above the river that gave the town its distinctive name.

Despite a typically eighteenth-century misspelling, the 1734 prospect set the stage for the drama of the beginnings of Savannah. One of the most exceptional bird's-eye views made during George II's reign, it perfectly illustrated the Trustees' aspirations as they attempted to settle a Spartan utopia on the fringes of the British Empire. The view showed a layout resembling an orderly series of London-like squares, but it also revealed the Spartan simplicities of Savannah such as identical rows of small frame cottages arranged like military barracks. In detail and overall spirit, Savannah was a Castrum encampment along the far frontiers of classical Rome.

Those in Georgian England who saw this view of a fortified embryo London knew the Georgia Trustees intended to create a utopia where deserving colonists "on the charity" might find refuge from poverty and persecution. A Georgia colonist who wrote back to London in 1735 described Savannah as "a promised land." For this needy colonist, an English Georgian town pared to essentials on the southernmost edge of the empire was indeed a "shining prospect." Nevertheless, to the south lay hostile Spanish Florida, and across the Savannah River to the north were the unaffordable sophistications of American Georgian life in low-country Carolina.

Savannah "as it stood the 29th of March 1734" is usually called The Peter Gordon View, after the First Bailiff of Savannah who arranged important aspects of the preparation of the engraving. A better name for the

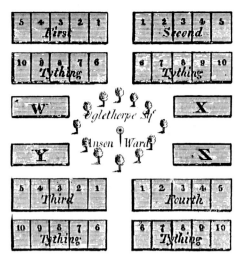

This detail, from a map by John McKinnon in 1820, shows Oglethorpe Square in the center of Anson Ward. The letters W, X, Y, and Z designate "Trust" lots reserved for public buildings. The four "Tything" lots were for settlers' cottages.

prospect might be The Oglethorpe-Gordon-Fourdrinier View, or simply The Trustees' View. "Dedicated to the Hon.[ble] the Trustees . . . by their Honours Obliged and Most Obedient Servant Peter Gordon," it was engraved in the summer of 1734 by Paul Fourdrinier, a master of his craft and part of a family of London engravers well known to Oglethorpe. In 1727 and 1728, Oglethorpe subscribed to two large and important folios Fourdrinier engraved for followers of Lord Burlington's English Palladian architectural revival: *The Designs of Inigo Jones* by William Kent, London, 1727, and *Villas of the Ancients Illustrated* by Robert Castell, London, 1728. (Appendix 1 discusses the connections between Oglethorpe, Castell, Fourdrinier, English Palladianism, the founding of Georgia, and the unique Savannah town plan.)

As with other aspects of the drama of founding the new colony, Oglethorpe—later General Oglethorpe—played a leading role in creating the first prospect view of Savannah. His association ensured a professionally engraved, elegant, and accurate representation, and the seemingly inexplicable date, "the 29th of March 1734," was his date of departure for London after a year in the colony. In late March 1734, Oglethorpe left Savannah for Charleston, South Carolina, to sail for London. He took the chief of the Yamacraw Indians, Tomochichi, and the chief's family and other tribesmen with him to introduce at the court of George II. Arriving in June 1734, Oglethorpe met with the king, his fellow Trustees, and Peter Gordon, his chief Savannah magistrate who had returned to London in February of that year. Gordon later recorded his meeting with Oglethorpe in a journal, one of many kept by those who helped found Georgia: "As soon as Mr. Oglethorpe arrived in England he gave me an account of what additional buildings had been raised since my coming away, and desired that I would have [the finished view] printed and dedicated to the Trustees" (1974, p. 36). Gordon had already shown the Trustees a sketch of Savannah; he wrote: "The Trustees . . . order'd me to gett a compleat drawing made . . . which I presented to them as soon as it was finished." Evidently Gordon had a topographical artist make a finished drawing that Oglethorpe inspected and revised to reflect the appearance of the town as it stood when he last saw it "the 29th of March." Oglethorpe then directed Gordon to have it engraved and printed.

Posterity has Oglethorpe to thank for the dramatic Fourdrinier engraving that recorded the Trustees' historic undertaking in America. It was a "shining prospect" of what Oglethorpe and the Trustees conceived as the appropriate nucleus for a Georgian town in the colony: a central square surrounded by places for public buildings, or "trust lots," and for settlers' cottages, or "tithing lots." An account in 1741 by a colonist named Patrick Tailfer was explicit and complimentary: "The Plan of the Town was beau-

P. Fourdrinier Sculp.
P. Gordon Inv.

tifully laid out in Wards, Tithings, and public Squares left at proper Distances for Markets and publick Buildings, the whole making an agreeable Uniformity" (1973, p. 109). The 1734 prospect showed four of these modules of wards, tithings, and public squares. Johnson Square, Derby Ward, the one most complete and occupied, is to the left in front of "Mr. Oglethorpe's Tent." (At the bottom of the view is a numbered key; Oglethorpe's tent is number 2.) The prospect depicted a far horizon extending into the public lands. Toward that horizon, from the original nucleus by the river, the modules of square and ward were repeated as the town expanded southward. By the 1850s there were twenty-four wards.

Every detail of the prospect was revealing. Almost centered in the view, Oglethorpe's tent alluded to his leadership of the undertaking: to his position as a British army officer and his interest in the military affairs of the colony and to his ability to "rough it" in the colony even though he was an esquire and a Trustee. By means of this prospect, Oglethorpe graphically demonstrated his preeminence, suggesting that his tent in front of the original embryo square was the source of order from which, according to plan, would come the eventual growth of the town and the success of the colony.

The obsession of Georgian England with town planning, especially the concept of residential squares, was fortunate for Savannah. The squares were typically open, orderly, healthy, and elegant. Oglethorpe's early correspondence to the Trustees in February 1733, referred to his selection of "a healthy situation, about Ten Miles from the Sea." He wrote: "The River here forms an Half-moon, along the South side of which the Banks are about Forty Feet high, and on the Top a Flat, which they call a Bluff. . . . Upon the River-side, in the Centre of this Plain, I have laid out the town" (1975, p.4). As the 1734 prospect displayed, the town was an interpretation of eighteenth-century English planning—a grid pattern of streets organized around central open spaces, as though several of the squares in London—Bloomsbury, St. James's and Hanover—were to be assembled on Yamacraw Bluff, a sandy *tabula rasa* "Upon the riverside." When Oglethorpe returned to England in 1743 for the last time, six of these units of squares and wards had been established. One of them bore his name. And Johnson Square, just off of Bay Street, with Bull Street forming the main north-south processional artery around the squares, had become the center of the plan, as it is today.

The Oglethorpe-Gordon-Fourdrinier View recorded the birth of this town plan that makes the historic district of Savannah the most Georgian city in America. The shining prospect that Savannah was in 1734 has become the reality of today. It is a prospect still full of hope and of course change, as it has been for more than 250 years. But it is still anchored in

Detail from the 1734 Trustees' View. Oglethorpe's tent is in the strand to the right of Bull Street and in front of Derby Ward, the first of the four original wards surveyed and settled. The ward consists of a square named for the Royal Governor of South Carolina, Robert Johnson; four trust lots; and four tythings of ten identical frame cottages on lots sixty feet by ninety feet, facing north to south across Johnson Square. This is the basic nucleus of the town plan. *Georgia Historical Society.*

the eighteenth-century heritage Georgian England bestowed. In time, the town, which Oglethorpe and the Trustees originally conceived of as a New World utopia, evolved into a lasting, very real, uniquely beautiful city with a diverse citizenry and an intense sense of history.

By means of other views, from a variety of eras, we will illustrate the changing scenes and prospects of a "Georgia Georgian" town like no other. The first glimpse London had of Savannah "as it stood the 29th of March 1734" has been ours. The next prospect, looking south from essentially the same vantage point, is a painting done by J. L. Firmin Cerveau in 1837, more than one hundred years later.

City views, called prospects in the eighteenth century, began to be called panoramas in the nineteenth. A local sign painter by trade, Cerveau painted a panorama perhaps a bit less professional than the London engraver's prospect, but it is a charming document of its time, a glimpse of Savannah "as it stood" in the spring of 1837. That year Queen Victoria was crowned; the present capital of Georgia, Atlanta, was founded as a railroad terminus in the Appalachian foothills; and the city fathers of Savannah, using more of the public lands set aside as commons by the Georgia Trustees, added three more of the basic units of Oglethorpe's town plan: Madison Square, Jasper Ward and Lafayette and Pulaski squares, with wards bearing the name of their central squares. This made eighteen squares—fourteen since the original four shown in the 1734 prospect. Cerveau, however, showed open common land south of Liberty Street where those three new wards were developed. He depicted a town of about ten thousand from East Broad to West Broad, Liberty to Bay.

Both the early eighteenth-century engraving and the early nineteenth-century painting of Savannah illustrated a place with promise, with "shining prospects." The 1734 view showed the bare bones of a "Georgia Georgian" town projected southward into the public lands in an orderly manner. By 1837, this was literally fleshed out with numerous wards and squares to the south, as well as to the east and west. The founders of Savannah could only have been pleased by the attractive appearance of the town one hundred years later.

Cerveau viewed the town from the bell tower of the late-eighteenth-century City Exchange, which stood on Bay Street at the head of Bull Street (until City Hall replaced it in 1905). As a result of the growth in Savannah, the scene Cerveau captured in his springtime panorama of 1837 was shifted slightly to the left or east of the one drawn in 1734. Then Whitaker Street symmetrically divided four squares: Johnson from Ellis and Wright from Telfair. By 1837, however, Bull Street and Johnson Square formed the central spine of the symmetrical plan that filled the riverside of Yamacraw Bluff: Ellis, sometimes called Market Square, on the

A panorama of Savannah on a spring morning as painted in 1837 by Firmin Cerveau (1812–1896), a commercial artist. Cerveau's view looked south down Bull Street with Johnson Square in the middle ground and Bay Street in the foreground. He depicted a town of about ten thousand, from East Broad to West Broad and Bay Street to Liberty Street. (The picture, 49½″ wide and 27½″ tall, hangs at the Georgia Historical Society, Savannah.)

west and Reynolds Square, created in 1742, on the east. In the foreground at the edge of the bluff was Bay Street, and near the absolute center of the scene was the white marble obelisk in Johnson Square. The area across Bay Street where Oglethorpe's tent had stood in the 1734 prospect did not show. (This area is now within a strand of public land called Emmett Park.)

Cerveau's view of the Savannah townscape 103 years after Fourdrinier's prospect also did not include the river and wharves, which were the focus of the cotton trade and thus the location of much of the commercial life in the town. Cerveau emphasized leisure and social life. Nevertheless, he alluded to the beginnings of the railroad services that brought upland cotton to the port—on the far edge of town a Central of Georgia railway engine puffs in from the west.

After Eli Whitney perfected the cotton gin on a nearby plantation in 1793, Savannah began to be a tremendously busy port. From 1830 through 1850, the railroad accelerated that prosperous activity, and Savannah became a low-country "capital" with a well-to-do society led by a cotton-merchant elite highly influenced by England and Englishmen. Cerveau recognized something of the commerce in town by including the row of buildings fronting along the south side of Bay Street. This brick, commercial row to the right of Bull Street, with arched and fanlighted doorways, could have been anywhere in the English-speaking world: London or Liverpool; New York, Philadelphia, or Baltimore.

In 1837, town officials began to fence, plant, and sometimes dress up the squares with handsome memorials. Coming to an end was the era when squares were multipurpose open spaces, as they had been in the early eighteenth-century fortified village organized like an ancient military encampment. The tall obelisk in the center of Johnson Square, designed by Philadelphia architect William Strickland, was at that time dedicated to two Revolutionary heroes: Casimir Pulaski, who now has his own memorial in Monterey Square, and to Nathanael Greene, whose monument alone this is today. (As Savannah evolved, the placement of memorials was not usually coordinated with the name of squares and wards, and this can be perplexing. The Greene Monument is in Johnson instead of Greene Square; the Pulaski Monument is in Monterey rather than Pulaski Square; and the Oglethorpe Monument is in Chippewa rather than Oglethorpe Square.)

Cerveau's panorama captured the proliferation of residential squares, tree-shaded, spacious, and bordered by dignified brick houses of two and three stories which overlooked the squares or were in sight of them from the grid pattern of streets. He depicted a town with a resemblance to the Georgian squares of the West End of London, a "Georgia Georgian" place with romantic Southern appeal that captivated travelers. In 1839, an En-

This detail of Cerveau's painting shows a three-story brick commercial row on West Bay Street and, on the far right, the City Hotel, at that time the most fashionable hostelry in Savannah.

glish travel writer, James Silk Buckingham, wrote: "There are no less than eighteen squares, with green plats and trees, in the very heart of the city, disposed at equal distances from each other in the greatest order" (1973, p. 137). In 1858, another Englishman, Charles Mackay, described the assemblage of parklike squares in Savannah in *Sketches of a Tour:* "Of all the cities in America none impresses itself more vividly upon the imagination and the memory than this little green bowery city of the South" (1859, p. 334). That was when Savannah began to be called "The Forest City," its longtime sobriquet.

Savannah had suffered, though, despite the impression Cerveau gave of a prosperous Southern oasis, a carefree little city with none but "shining prospects." During the Revolution, the British occupied Savannah, and, between the prospect of 1734 and the 1837 panorama, the town had had two calamitous fires, in 1796 and 1820, which were worse than the Revolutionary War. The panorama showed a major relic of the 1820 conflagration, the rear of a burnt-out shell on Bryan Street east of Bull Street ("lot number nine Jekyl Tything"), opposite the Bank of the State of Georgia, in the middle left of the view. This was the ruin of a two-story brick customhouse designed, as well as constructed, by the brilliant young British architect William Jay. Jay was a native of Bath, England, who came to Savannah in 1817 as the designer of a house for Richard Richardson on Oglethorpe Square (now the Owens-Thomas Museum). Before the fire and yellow fever epidemic of 1820, Jay was responsible for several handsome mansions, a branch bank of the United States, a theater, possibly a hotel (the City Hotel in the lower right corner of The Cerveau View), and this customhouse, which Savannah historians heretofore have not recognized as his work. Research in the course of preparing the manuscript for this book produced several government documents that proved Jay's authorship. A contract dated 27 May 1819 recorded: "A Brick building intended to be used as a Custom House according to the plans . . . by William Jay" (National Archives). Another document, dated 1842, described William Jay as the "contractor" and added: "The custom-house, when nearly completed, was destroyed by an extensive conflagration, which occurred in Savannah in the year 1820" (Author's collection). It was the first United States customhouse built as such in Savannah, and the detail in Cerveau's panorama is presumably the only graphic evidence of its almost forgotten existence.

The town of Savannah in the eighteenth and early nineteenth centuries was built largely of wood, and much of that construction was destroyed in the fires of 1796 and 1820. One survivor was the old Filature, or silk house, a remnant of the Trustees' attempt to grow silk in Savannah in the earlier days of the colony. Located on the northeast trust lot of Reynolds

Cerveau detail showing the ruin of the United States Custom House on East Bryan Street. This building, designed by William Jay and begun in 1819, burned in the great fire of January 11, 1820.

The old Filature, or silk house, on the northeast trust lot of Reynolds Square. This structure, once also used as the city hall, was a relic of the simple frame buildings from the Trustees' era and a reminder of their frustrated attempts to sponsor the production of silk. It survived from the colonial period until two years after Cerveau painted this view.

Detail from the 1734 Trustees' View. Oglethorpe is believed to have stayed in this cottage, at the southeast corner of Bay and Bull streets, after leaving his tent for more substantial quarters. This same cottage, later enlarged, may be the shop on East Bay Street in the Cerveau panorama. Today, it is the site of the United States Custom House.

"The Lott for the Church," Johnson Square, Derby Ward, from the 1734 engraving. Christ Episcopal Church has occupied this trust lot since the eighteenth century.

Square, it served at one point as the city hall and did not burn until 1839. In Cerveau's painting, this remnant of the numerous eighteenth-century frame buildings of Savannah was nestled at the left edge among the trees of Reynolds Square to the east of the customhouse ruins. Another frame survivor of the great fires, and of the years since Oglethorpe's sojourn in Savannah, was a cottage believed to be one of those shown in the 1734 prospect. Enlarged and converted into a shop with two wide display windows, it stood on the southeast corner of Bull and Bay where the granite customhouse of 1852 stands today. (This cottage has been thought to be where Oglethorpe, after he had given up his tent, rented a room whenever he was in Savannah.)

In the 1734 bird's-eye view, on Johnson Square there were four trust lots facing across the open space east to west: number 9 was "The Lott for the Church." In The Cerveau View, that lot had been used for its intended purpose. Christ Episcopal Church, as it looked in 1837 with its brick edifice of the late-Georgian period, stood out with its prominent classical belfry. (In 1838, because of a structural failure, this building was taken down completely and rebuilt in the classical revival style; except for certain details, it is essentially the church one sees on Johnson Square today.) In 1837, next to the Christ Church lot, where "The publick Stores" had stood in 1734 (number 10 in the prospect), was a bank, as there is today. The Bank of the State of Georgia is recorded from the second story up—a late-Georgian, Adam or Federal style, two-story brick structure with large fanlight windows, a parapet and four chimneys, looking almost like a private residence. Designed by a carpenter-architect from New England, as were many Savannah buildings, it was demolished in 1905.

Trust lots, a special characteristic of the Savannah version of the Georgian period townscape, came to figure greatly in the architecture of important dwellings in Savannah, as well as in that of the public buildings which they were, in theory, originally laid out to accommodate and display. On these desirable lots, three great houses by William Jay and two by the New York architect John S. Norris were sited: William Jay's Richardson-Owens-Thomas; Bulloch-Habersham (destroyed c. 1915); and Telfair (now Telfair Academy of Arts and Sciences); and John Norris's Andrew Low and Charles Green houses. Trust lots allowed a three-dimensional display of all elevations including a glimpse of garden façades in deep rear gardens extending all the way to the next cross street. (Four of the museum houses in the following section, the Jay and Norris houses noted here, were built in Trust lots.)

From 1837 until the onset of the Civil War in 1861, prospects for Savannah seemed to shine more each year. Expanding toward Gaston Street on the south, six more squares and wards were added and one place, or

Christ Episcopal Church, Johnson Square, as it appeared in 1837, before it was rebuilt in the classic Greek Revival style of the present church.

22

Lithograph by Charles Parsons (1821-1910) after a drawing by John William Hill, 1855, 27¹¹⁄₁₆ × 39¹⁵⁄₁₆ in., from Monterey Square looking north toward the river and the City Exchange (site of the present city hall). Monterey Ward dates from 1847, and the Pulaski Monument, in the center of the square, was completed in January 1855. To the left of the monument is a brick house on the corner of Bull and West Taylor streets. It is a typical Savannah dwelling built for the prosperous classes of the 1850s, with two stories on a high basement, the parlor floor reached by a flight of steps rising from a sandy sidewalk, and an enclosed garden with parterres. In the same year that this lithograph was printed, William Makepeace Thackeray described Savannah as "a tranquil old city, wide-streeted, tree-planted, with a few cows and carriages toiling through the sandy road" (1887, p. 169). *Private Collection*.

Detail from the 1837 Cerveau panorama. The Federal style Bank of the State of Georgia, built in 1819 by a carpenter-architect from Maine, stood on the northeast trust lot of Johnson Square. Below the bank and to the right Cerveau has added the charming detail of life in the lane between Bryan and Bay streets. Most of the lanes have survived modern growth, and although today one rarely sees cows and horses, as depicted in this vignette, these quiet avenues provide convenient access to stores in the business district and a pleasant respite from street-front living in the residential area.

23

Photograph from about 1895, looking south down Bull Street toward Johnson and Wright squares. Church spires are the tallest forms on the horizon and few structures are taller than three or four stories. The Screven House, to the right of Christ Episcopal Church, is the tallest building. The scale of Savannah remained in 1895 much as it had been in the Cerveau panorama of 1837, and there are no motor cars. *Georgia Historical Society.*

Photograph, c. 1893, showing Factors' Row and Walk and the strand, on the north side of East Bay Street. Although Savannah is still one of the busiest ports on the south Atlantic, most of the shipping activity is now conducted up-river. Buildings such as Stoddard's Upper Range and the Cotton Exchange have been saved, however, and now stand as vivid reminders of the commerce that shaped the lives and the architecture of the old city. *Georgia Historical Society.*

park, and ward. With one exception, Whitefield Square, Wesley Ward, 1851, the names of these central squares and those of their wards were the same: Crawford Square, 1841; Monterey Square, 1847; Chatham Square, 1847; Troup Square, 1851; Calhoun Square, 1851; and Forsyth Place, later Park, and ward, 1851. South of Gaston Street, later in the 1850s, several new wards were added without central squares; Forsyth Place served as a central park for that area of town. Thus, after 125 years, the original town plan, except for the grid pattern of streets, ceased to be used.

In 1860, on the eve of the Civil War, the population of Savannah was 22,292: 13,875 citizens and 8,417 non-whites. During the three antebellum decades prior to this, as direct trade with England became more and more important and cotton became king, some of the leading citizens in Savannah were not Georgians at all, but subjects of Queen Victoria; among these English cotton merchants and factors were Andrew Low, William Battersby, Charles Green, and Edward Molyneux. Their homes were mansions that could have graced a London square, and their warehouses, wharves, and factors' walk offices along the bay front teemed with activity. And Savannah remained, in spirit and physical appearance, the Georgian town it had become before and after the American Revolution.

By the 1850s, the style of Savannah was formed. It was a distinctively local expression of Georgian taste that had evolved in its semitropical latitude: on wide, tree-lined streets intersected at regular intervals by spacious parks and squares stood houses of brick, often of a brown-grey local variety, sometimes covered with tan stucco—dignified houses on high basements, with lofty rooms of parlor or main floors lighted by large shuttered windows and reached from high stoops; houses with main living areas raised into the tree tops above the hot, dusty streets. This "Georgia Georgian" picture was completed by handsome ironwork and half-hidden gardens—a setting of restrained charm arranged in an orderly, harmonious fashion on the town lots, sixty by ninety feet, or some proportion thereof, which Oglethorpe originally blocked out in 1733.

At the end of, and after, the Civil War, Savannah remained physically much the same, for, even though it suffered blockade and occupation in 1864, it was neither bombarded nor put to Sherman's torch. Obviously society had to make some essential adjustments to a new order, but, in matters of architecture, interiors, and gardens, its fundamentally British heritage persisted within the old wards around the historic squares. A photographic view of Savannah in 1893 showed a place little different in scale and overall appearance from the panorama Cerveau painted fifty-six years earlier. In 1886, Will Glazier, writing in *Peculiarities of American Cities*, described Savannah as "the most beautiful city of the South, if not the United States. It is more like the wealthy suburb of some large city, than

Photograph from the 1930s, looking south on Bull Street from the city hall. In the 1920s and 1930s, motor cars and skyscrapers dominated the city scene, changing the scale and appearance of Savannah as nothing had done for some two hundred years. Savannah remained a "forest city" because of the series of planted squares and medians, but paving had replaced the sand underfoot and tall buildings the spires on the horizon. Hotels and office buildings dwarfed the Nathanael Greene obelisk and the live oaks of Johnson Square. *Georgia Historical Society.*

like a city itself. It is embowered in trees, which are green the whole year around" (p. 478).

Only in the early twentieth century did major changes dramatically alter the old prospect of graceful Georgian-style church spires rising above a "Forest City" on the banks of a tidal river. Two-, three-, and four-story brick buildings began to be replaced by shiny new skyscrapers—the twentieth-century version of "shining prospects."

Tall buildings with elevators, however, were not the only changes that came in with the new century. The motor car also brought changes in the configuration of Savannah, making suburbs convenient. Some of these suburbs are today recognized as historic districts in their own right. Although they are of less age and extent than the large National Historic Landmark District, they are now more than fifty years of age and have a special character that lends an additional spectrum of interest outside of the area shown in Cerveau's panorama.

After the Civil War and into the twentieth century, these suburbs were developed as Savannah expanded southward—away from the river that gave the town its name, witnessed its founding, and encouraged its initial growth. Savannahians began to move away from the tree-shaded squares lined with the historic, visually pleasing mix of private, public, and commercial buildings that had formerly constituted the whole of the town. At the turn of the century, street cars and "horseless carriages" helped this process along, as new suburbs continued to be formed beyond the old wards from the farm lands that were south of Gaston and Gwinnett Streets and Forsyth Park. Savannahians even took up permanent residence at historic resort villages on the tidewater rivers and marshes east of town, as some few had done in antebellum days.

As this happened, Savannahians left behind them the rich but increasingly sad and romantically moldering evidence of the eighteenth- and nineteenth-century civilization their ancestors had created. In effect, the entire old city became a landmark, a decidedly unique landmark, which began to deteriorate in the 1920s and 1930s, continuing into the immediate post–World War II years. Individual monuments of the architecture of that older civilization began to disappear; even squares were threatened, and several were lost in the path of highways. One became the site of a parking garage. Much survived, however, and the extraordinary urban plan—an eighteenth-century gift from England to America—continued to give Savannah a special sense of cohesion, even as the city seemed to be falling apart. Some of the best examples of domestic architecture were destroyed, yet many were saved by restoring them as museums. The museum houses that follow were the first fruits of the efforts to preserve and enhance a classic place—the Georgia Georgian City of Savannah.

River Street and the bay front from Hutchinson's Island.

Isaiah Davenport House, 1820, 324 East
State Street, Columbia Square.

Alexander Telfair House, after it had become the Telfair Academy, c. 1890. *Georgia Historical Society.*

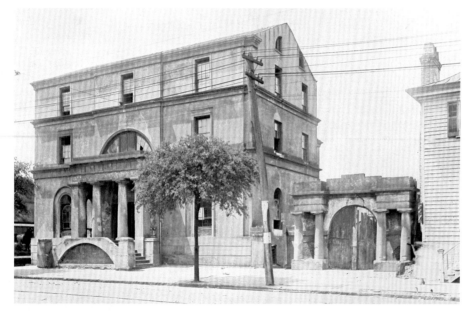

William Scarbrough House. The third story was removed during the restoration of the 1970s. *Georgia Historical Society.*

Richard Richardson House (Owens-Thomas Museum), photographed from Oglethorpe Square, c. 1880. *Georgia Historical Society.*

The Museum Houses

SAVANNAHIANS HAVE LOVINGLY preserved seven houses as museums that represent classic pre–Civil War architecture, interiors, and gardens and capture vivid glimpses of pre-twentieth-century life, history, and culture.

Built from the 1810s through the 1850s, in several instances enlarged in the 1880s and 1890s, these houses were restored and renovated in our own century. Each is a museum in some sense and open to the public regularly. Only three are in the fullest sense "house museums," solely serving that educational purpose: the Davenport, Owens-Thomas, and Andrew Low houses; but all function to some degree as "restorations," with their architecture, interiors, and gardens acting as exhibits in and of themselves.

The Telfair House became the Telfair Museum of Arts and Sciences in the 1880s, with gallery space and other alterations by a noted New York architect, Detlef Lienau. Some of its rooms have been restored to their original appearance and appropriately furnished; in 1981–82, for example, the octagonal Oak Room was restored to the way it was c. 1820 in Alexander Telfair's day. Architecturally, the Scarbrough House has been restored, including removal of mid-nineteenth century and later changes. It is the headquarters of the Historic Savannah Foundation, Inc. The atrium and some of the other main rooms have been restored to represent the era of William Scarbrough, who had the house built in 1819, and of his English-born architect William Jay.

William Jay's neoclassical architecture is well represented among these houses; three are definitely attributed to him: the Telfair, Owens-Thomas, and Scarbrough houses. The Wayne-Gordon House, where Juliette Magill Gordon (Low) was born in 1860, is also usually said to be his design. With additions from the 1880s still intact, it is known as the Juliette Gordon Low Girl Scout National Center. Much of the house is open to visitors and furnished as Juliette Gordon knew it when she lived there before her marriage in 1886 to William Mackay Low of Savannah and London, England, son of Andrew Low, whose house is also a museum.

Front hall, Isaiah Davenport House, Historic American Buildings Survey, mid-1930s. *Library of Congress.*

Isaiah Davenport House as photographed by the Historic American Buildings Survey, mid-1930s. *Library of Congress.*

Green-Meldrim House, Madison Square, photographed about 1900, when it was Judge Peter Meldrim's residence. Smooth stucco, scored to simulate stone, was the original exterior finish. *Georgia Historical Society*.

The Andrew Low House is one of two of these houses designed by a New York architect, John S. Norris, who worked in Savannah during the 1840s and 1850s, the other is the Green-Meldrim House. Norris's biographer, Mary Lane Morrison, has described him as "an eclectic virtuoso who designed in a blend of many styles." Both houses clearly demonstrate her evaluation. The Low House is a full-time house museum, but it also functions as Georgia headquarters for the National Society of Colonial Dames. The Green-Meldrim House, in somewhat the same way, is the parish house for St. John's Episcopal Church with main rooms especially furnished and open to the public. The gardens of both houses have survived in their original forms, green parterres separated by gravel walks, two of only a handful of mid-nineteenth-century Savannah gardens remaining.

One additional house, an eighth that may become a museum, is the classical revival Champion-McAlpin House, left to a national patriotic society in 1985 by Alida Harper Fowlkes, an early leader of historic preservation efforts in the Savannah Historic District. Designed by Charles B. Cluskey and built in 1842, it had a third floor added in 1895. It is located on the southeast trust lot of Orleans Square.

Some of the grand houses of early Savannah are no longer standing. Victims of fire, neglect, and the pressures of modernization, they exist only in sketchy descriptions and faded photographs. These images are frustrating records, but vivid reminders, of the great effort Savannahians have made to preserve the museum houses that follow.

The Telfair became an art museum in the last quarter of the nineteenth century. Thereafter, the houses became museums in 1928 (Low), 1942 (Green-Meldrim), 1951 (Owens-Thomas), 1953 (Wayne-Gordon), 1955 (Davenport), and 1973 (Scarbrough). Much of what Savannah values about its past is embodied in the old bricks, stucco, and tabby of these houses; together they constitute a fine panorama of classic Savannah architecture, interiors, and gardens.

Champion-McAlpin House, west elevation, overlooking Orleans Square. Designed by Charles B. Cluskey in 1844 for Aaron Champion, it is the last great house remaining on Orleans Square. It was bequeathed to a national organization in 1985.

Champion-McAlpin House as it appeared in *Art Work of Savannah*, 1893, before the third story was added later in the 1890s. *Georgia Historical Society.*

Archibald Bulloch House, Orleans Square, 1818-1819. This mansion, designed by William Jay, is one of the more notable examples of Savannah architecture lost to the wrecking crews. It was demolished about 1915. *Georgia Historical Society.*

Robert Habersham House, c. 1819, Orleans Square. William Jay may have also designed this house, which closely resembles the William Scarbrough House. Like the Bulloch House, the Habersham House has also been demolished, however, and the Champion-McAlpin House now stands alone as a reminder of the grandeur of nineteenth-century Orleans Square. Savannahians have expended great effort and resources on the restorations featured in this section, for without this commitment, our only experience with any of these fascinating houses might be through melancholy photographs like these. *Georgia Historical Society.*

South elevation, East State Street, overlooking Columbia Square.

ISAIAH DAVENPORT HOUSE

1820–1821, Columbia Square, 325 East State Street

IT IS WELL TO BEGIN with the Isaiah Davenport House, because it has become the symbol of restoration in Savannah. Although several of the houses that follow were already museums in 1955 when this house was scheduled for destruction, its narrow escape and successful restoration provided fresh impetus for historic preservation in Savannah. From this prominent site facing Columbia Square on the north side of Columbia Ward, a new resolve grew to protect and restore the classic beauty of the historic architecture and plan of Georgian Savannah.

Columbia Square and Ward date from 1799 when Savannah spread east and west into public lands on either side of the original six squares and wards laid out by James Oglethorpe. That same year Isaiah Davenport (1784–1827) left his home in Rhode Island to immigrate to Savannah, where he would prosper as a builder-architect. Davenport married Sara Clark in 1809, and in 1818 he was elected an alderman and began constructing his residence on Columbia Square.

In the prosperous years after the Revolutionary War, talented people like Davenport arrived in Savannah ready to build as they had back home, but their Georgian style assumed a slightly new accent. Sitting right at the sidewalk on one of the building lots of restricted size the town plan dictated and on a high basement the unpaved, dusty streets required, Davenport's dignified, well-proportioned, two-story brick house summed up the American Georgian style as it developed in the southern port during the first decades of the nineteenth century.

In 1955, when the house was a tenement and about to be dismantled for its fine building materials and valuable corner site, it was saved by a small group of public-spirited citizens who incorporated Historic Savannah Foundation. Many of the historic preservation successes evolved from the efforts of those original stalwarts of Savannah. A major achievement occurred in 1966 when the old planned city of wards and squares was designated a National Historic Landmark District.

Restored and furnished, the Isaiah Davenport House was headquarters for Historic Savannah Foundation, Inc., until the William Scarbrough House became a similar project for the foundation in the 1970s. Still owned by Historic Savannah, the Davenport House is regularly open to

Entrance hall. An arched screen of Ionic columns adorns the asymmetrical hall. The original iron work can be seen on the porch.

Parlor detail.

Parlor. Davenport's skills as a carpenter-architect are displayed throughout the parlor floor. Ionic columns connected by segmental arches are the dominant ornament. A Jeremiah Theus (c. 1719–1774) portrait of Miss Brailsford, c. 1770, hangs over a neoclassical marble mantelpiece, which is original to the house.

Dining room. Windows on either side of a replacement mantel offer a view of the garden on the west side of the house.

the public and exemplifies one of those dwellings in Savannah that James Silk Buckingham, an Englishman traveling in America in 1839, described in these oft-quoted words: "The greater number of dwelling-houses are built of wood, and painted white; but there are many handsome and commodious brick buildings occupied as private residences . . . which are of beautiful architecture, of sumptuous interior, and combine as much of elegance and luxury as are to be found in any private dwellings in the country." (1973, p. 138).

In that same description, Buckingham also mentioned "a few mansions, built by an English architect, Mr. Jay." William Jay, a brilliant young architect, arrived in Savannah about the time Isaiah Davenport, an established builder, began this fine residence on Columbia Square. Mr. Davenport's classic architectural statement of "Savannah, Georgia, Georgian" is followed in the next pages by four of Mr. Jay's "mansions' that added a taste of George IV's English Regency to the established scene.

37

West elevation, Abercorn Street, overlooking Oglethorpe Square.

RICHARD RICHARDSON HOUSE

1819, Owens-Thomas Museum
Oglethorpe Square, 124 Abercorn Street

THIS TRULY EXTRAORDINARY HOUSE stands on the northeast trust lot of Oglethorpe Square, in the sixth and last ward laid out during James Oglethorpe's stay in the colony. Anson Ward, named for Lord George Anson, Admiral of the Fleet in the 1720s and 1730s, dates from 1742 and Oglethorpe Square from the same year. Between 1816 and 1819, Richard Richardson had the house built as his residence. It is now called the Owens-Thomas Museum.

Richard Richardson was a banker and cotton merchant whose wife Frances Bolton was related by marriage to the young architect William Jay(1792–1837), a native of Bath, England. Richardson commissioned Jay to design the house even though Jay was twenty-five years old and living in London. The youthful architect's Englishness, however, probably recommended him to the Savannah cotton broker, and the London-like residential squares of Savannah would have sparked the imagination of the youthful Briton, as we have abundant evidence.

William Jay arrived in December 1817 after the house was under construction and stayed several years, designing and building some of the most distinguished structures in town, including a branch bank of the United States for its president Richard Richardson, and a customhouse that burned in the Fire of 1820.

Jay is thought to have sent the house design from England, and it undoubtedly reflects his fine background and training in Regency England. Just as Isaiah Davenport had learned his craft in Federal-period New England and yet built a home for himself on Columbia Square that perfectly suited Savannah, William Jay's design for Richard Richardson well suits its Savannah trust lot. Even so, the design suggests the Regency villas of his native Bath, with its warm stucco exterior, sinuous classical revival entrance, and delightfully arranged and ornamented interior. Only one

Balcony, south elevation. William Jay advocated cast iron as a building material and used it here to create the finest Regency verandah in America.

Vestibule and central stair hall. A screen of columns with gilded Greek Corinthian capitals frames the dramatic staircase.

Staircase and bridge. Crafted like a piece of inlaid Regency furniture, an intricate staircase rises in the center of the house, reminiscent of the architecture of the English neoclassicists Sir Robert Taylor and Sir John Soane. An arched bridge connects the front upstairs hall to the rear.

Reception room, or parlor. This room is most like the Regency architecture of Sir John Soane, whose work Jay admired. The ceiling, with corner spandrels like gathered cloth and the concentric circles of Greek frets, make the square room seem circular, in the manner of Soane's own house in London. The classical marble mantelpiece is original to the room.

Dining room, or north parlor. William Jay used Greek architectural details throughout his design. The projecting cornice of plaster anthemia is similar to that on the south verandah. The unusual shallow niche is Soanesque. The glass Greek key design permits an accent of indirect light on the north wall, and the Regency console has a marble top with a pedestal of mahogany and ebony.

Basement kitchen. The foundation is constructed of tabby, a local form of concrete made from equal parts of oyster shell, oyster-shell lime, and sand.

square apart and built at the same time, Davenport's and Richardson's houses are stylistically different but close cousins in the distinctive Georgian culture that grew up in the beguiling geometry of the squares on Yamacraw Bluff.

Richardson's Regency villa was William Jay's inaugural design for Savannah. Good times, however, came to an end soon for both architect and client due to depression, fire, and yellow fever. In 1822, Frances Bolton Richardson died and Richardson lost the house to creditors; at the same time, Jay departed Savannah for Charleston, South Carolina, where he worked until he left America permanently in 1822 to return to his homeland. In 1830, a leading Savannah citizen, George Welchman Owens, purchased the property after it had become the respectable boarding house of a Mrs. Maxwell who boarded the Marquis de Lafayette here in 1825 on his American tour.

In 1951, Owens's granddaughter, Miss Margaret Thomas, willed the house to the Telfair Academy of Arts and Sciences to become a museum honoring her father and grandfather. Of all Jay's surviving designs, it is the most complete house museum. It captures the spirit of early nineteenth-century Savannah as described by the British traveler James Silk Buckingham, for it is indeed "of beautiful architecture and sumptuous interior [combining] elegance and luxury" (1973, p. 138).

In the ongoing program to preserve and restore the authentic beauty and significance of the house, researchers have uncovered an unusually sophisticated system of cisterns and other plumbing. The restoration of lost features from that basic amenity is part of a long-range plan for recreating every original detail of a comfortable, convenient, and elegant villa, which is a National Historic Landmark open to the public daily.

Garden. The Regency style of this parterre garden in the former stable yard dates from the restoration in the early 1950s. The house, walled garden, and carriage house take up the entire trust lot.

WILLIAM SCARBROUGH HOUSE

1819, Historic Savannah Foundation, Inc.
41 West Broad Street

IN DECEMBER 1818, as this house was under construction, a Savannah merchant, Petit De Villers, wrote to General Charles Cotesworth Pinckney of South Carolina, "You would be astonished to see the number of handsome fire-proof dwelling houses . . . that are now erecting. . . .There are several houses here that would be an ornament to any city." One year before, in December 1817, William Jay arrived in Savannah and began erecting a series of houses that would indeed ornament Savannah. Those that survive decorate the city even to this day; and certainly they appeared fireproof, among them this house designed by Jay.

In May 1819, the next spring, William and Julia Scarbrough's house was virtually completed in time for a visit from President James Monroe on his southern tour. Scarbrough, like Richard Richardson, a "merchant prince" who lost his fortune in the 1820s, was a principal backer of the steamship *Savannah*, the first to cross the Atlantic; Monroe inspected the vessel and attended a reception in Scarbrough's new house. In a letter Scarbrough described his house as an expression of William Jay's "pure and genuine Taste." He also wrote: "Our house is quite in readiness [for the President]. It is most tastefully and elegantly decorated and furnished" (Lerski 1983, p. 89). (Some of the furnishings for the presidential visit were borrowed from neighbors.)

Only months after these happy occasions, however, in January 1820 a great fire destroyed the commercial center of the city, as well as hundreds of valuable houses. But this house and the Davenport, Richardson, and Telfair houses—all new or still being built—survived, perhaps because they were out of the direct path of the fire, rather than because of fireproof construction methods. Soon after this multi-million-dollar conflagration, William Jay published his professional services and proposed cast-iron as an alternative to timber. Jay wrote: "When we recollect how many brick buildings occupied the heart of the city, our astonishment is excited that they were destroyed, for they were deemed fireproof" (Lerski 1983, p. 51). (Jay did not mention his brick United States Custom House, almost completed on East Bryan Street at Johnson Square, which did burn and stood as a ruin until 1839.)

The William Scarbrough House is on the western edge of the historic district in what is now a commercial area, the last great house to occupy that neighborhood. Unlike the preceding three houses, it faces a thoroughfare rather than a square. In architectural form and style, it resembles the Telfair House, a villa in the newly fashionable Greek Revival style with the flavor of the restrained English-Regency neoclassicism that Jay introduced to Savannah. And, as with the Telfair House, major alterations were made to it later in the century, including the addition of an attic story.

Similarly this house had become a public building, a school, about the time the Telfair House became an art museum. After the school closed, the house deteriorated further, and not until the 1970s was it selected to become a museum and headquarters house, at which time the attic story was removed and other extensive restorations were made.

In 1977, the house was opened to the public with certain sections set aside as the working headquarters of Historic Savannah Foundation, Inc. The William Scarbrough House has been designated a National Historic Landmark.

East elevation, West Broad Street. William Jay designed this neoclassical villa for William Scarbrough, a Savannah cotton merchant and one of the owners of the S.S. *Savannah*, the first steamship to cross the Atlantic. The Scarbroughs entertained President Monroe in their new home before the inaugural voyage of the *Savannah* in May 1819.

Entrance hall, or atrium. This two-story galleried hall supported by four Doric columns resembles an atrium design of Regency taste-maker Thomas Hope in *Household Furniture* *and Interior Decoration* (1807). The *faux marbre* restoration was done in 1982.

Atrium skylight. As if the atrium were open to the heavens, this barrel-vaulted, sky-blue ceiling originally was painted with clouds, stars, and planets.

49

East elevation, Barnard Street, overlooking Telfair Square.

ALEXANDER TELFAIR HOUSE

c. 1820 and c. 1883
Telfair Academy of Arts and Sciences
Telfair Square, 121 Barnard Street

BUILT WITHIN MONTHS of the Davenport and Richardson houses—each today a house museum—the Telfair House by William Jay survives, with some alterations, as the front portion of the Telfair Academy of Arts and Sciences. In 1875, Mary Telfair, Alexander Telfair's sister and the last member of the Telfair family, bequeathed the home with its art collection, furnishings, "books, papers, and documents" to the Savannah Historical Society to administer. It was the first house in Savannah to be designated and preserved as a museum.

The Telfair House remained virtually intact until the 1880s when it was remodeled and enlarged to function as an art museum. The architect for this expansion was a noted New Yorker, the German-born Detlef Lienau, who had trained in Paris with Labrouste. Working with Carl N. Brandt, the first director of the Telfair Academy (also German-born), Lienau retained something of the character and details of William Jay's architecture, inside and out, while adding an attic story, a three-story west wing on the rear—containing a sculpture gallery and rotunda—and, at the entrance, five large Viennese stone statues representing Culture, flanking Jay's Greek Corinthian portico. The new museum, a combination of Jay's classical revival and Lienau's Renaissance eclecticism, was dedicated and opened in May 1886 and has continued to serve as the public art museum of the city, the oldest facility of this kind in the southeast.

One of Lienau's and Brandt's major interior changes to Jay's design was in the two-story entrance hall. They replaced a wooden stairway, similar to that in the Richardson House, with one of marble and installed at the second floor ceiling a series of plaster casts of the "Elgin Marbles" creating a Parthenon frieze, lighted by a skylight. The octagonal library-receiving room and dining room on the south and the double drawing rooms, or parlors, on the north remained essentially unchanged in form.

Reception room. Alexander Telfair's octagonal reception room, which he called the Oak Room, was restored and furnished in 1981–1982. Some of the *faux bois* surfaces had survived behind bookcases in the niches, and, with that evidence, the oak-grained plaster walls were recreated as designed by Jay. The furnishings are primarily nineteenth-century American. A pair of c. 1800 globes are Telfair family items. The gilt-bronze oil chandelier is original to the house.

Dining room. The carpet and the Monuments of Paris wallpaper are reproductions and were installed during restoration work in 1985. The room is filled with original Telfair furniture, including the large round dining table, maple chairs, and gilt-embellished sideboard.

Gallery detail. The long gallery at the Telfair mansion was originally divided into two parlors by a screen of columns. This detail shows the northeast corner with the rich cornice, curved wall, and inset arch typical of Jay's architecture. The mantel was carved by John Frazee about 1818.

For many years, these main rooms were used as picture galleries with furnishings from the Telfair family, but in time they have been restored and recreated as they were in Alexander Telfair's day; an inventory of the contents of the house taken after his death in 1832 has been useful in the extensive research toward these historic house museum recreations. Among the Telfair family furnishings are marble mantelpieces carved by John Frazee (1790–1852) and still installed in the double parlors and dining room, a Federal period Sheraton style mahogany sofa, a mahogany sideboard of the Phyfe era, and a suite of curly maple furniture, neoclassical in style, consisting of two meridiennes, a table, and seventeen side chairs.

The father of Alexander (1792–1832) and Mary Telfair (1789–1875) was Edward Telfair (1743–1807), a Revolutionary patriot and early governor of Georgia. Recognizing the Telfair's many contributions to Savannah, the city in 1883 changed the name of the square on which their home was built (on the northwest trust lot) from St. James's—presumably named after the residential square in London—to Telfair. It is the central square of Heathcote Ward, the fourth and last of the wards Oglethorpe laid out in 1733 and named for George Heathcote, a "Trustee for Establishing the Colony of Georgia in America."

South elevation, Oglethorpe Avenue.

JAMES MOORE WAYNE HOUSE

1820; 1831; 1860; 1886; 1953–56
Juliette Gordon Low Birthplace and Center
Oglethorpe Avenue and Bull Street

JULIETTE GORDON LOW'S BIRTHPLACE has an interesting chronology—a lengthy list of significant events and dates—and a mystery. Was William Jay its original architect? The house, in its first form, was completed about 1820 for the jurist James Moore Wayne (1790–1867), at that time mayor of Savannah and later a United States Supreme Court Justice. Wayne sold it in 1831 to his niece and her husband, William Washington Gordon I (1796–1842), grandparents of Juliette (Daisy) Gordon, who was born here in 1860. In 1886, several years after Juliette's father, William Washington Gordon II (1834–1912), inherited the property, he commissioned the accomplished architect Detlef Lienau of New York City to add an attic story and a curved side piazza. Lienau also made other alterations to accommodate Gordon's large family and to prepare the house for the wedding of Juliette Magill Gordon in late December to William Mackay Low of Savannah and London, England. The property remained in the Gordon family until 1953 when the Girl Scouts of the U.S.A. purchased the house to restore as a memorial to the founder of girl scouting and as a center for girl scout activities.

Dedicated and opened to the public in 1956, the house is furnished to represent the era of Juliette Gordon's youth in the 1870s and 1880s before she married. The furnishings reflect the taste of her parents, William Washington Gordon II and Eleanor Lytle Kinzie (1835–1917), and many family things are still in the house, including the bed in which "Daisy" Gordon was born on Halloween 1860.

There is no mystery about whether William Jay designed the three preceding houses, two of which also had third stories added as the scale of life in Savannah grew larger from the 1820s to the 1880s. Evidence for Jay's having given this house its original form, however, is only conjectural,

Parterre garden and side piazza. The piazza dates from the 1886 renovation, and the garden was restored in the 1950s. The spire of the Independent Presbyterian Church is visible across broad, tree-lined Oglethorpe Avenue.

Parlor. The portrait of Juliette Gordon Low is a copy of the original, which is now in the National Portrait Gallery in Washington, D.C. It is one of the many handsome portraits on display throughout the house. The Empire sofa is decorated with carvings of eagles and dolphins.

Parlor and rear parlor. This view into the rear parlor emphasizes the exceptional neo-classical ornamentation in both rooms.

based mainly on stylistic and other architectural similarities between it and his known designs. Traditionally it is said to be one of Jay's and undoubtedly the original house, before the 1886 additions, reflects the influence of his Regency architecture on the buildings of Savannah.

The house stands at the corner of Bull Street and Oglethorpe Avenue, facing the historic Independent Presbyterian Church and the landscaped median of the avenue, in Percival Ward, just south of Wright Square. In Wright Square, a granite and limestone monument honoring William Washington Gordon I was erected in 1884 for his services to the city and state, as well as to the business community as founder and first president of the Central of Georgia Railroad. Percival Ward was the second of the earliest wards laid out in 1733; it was named for the president of the Georgia Trustees, the Rt. Honorable John Lord Viscount Percival (1683–1748), first earl of Egmont, who was almost as important as James Oglethorpe in the founding of Georgia.

The house and Girl Scout Center, a National Historic Landmark, is open regularly. The Andrew Low House, where Juliette Gordon Low resided when she founded girl scouting, follows. Architecturally it represents a new era in the development of the town; with it we leave William Jay and enter the era of another architect, John S. Norris.

Library. The furnishings of this parlor floor room reflect the period of the 1886 remodeling.

Dining room. Research established the wall color and other aspects of the decor; the furnishings are Gordon family pieces.

Southwest bedroom. This second floor bedroom has been restored with Juliette Gordon Low's furniture.

Southeast bedroom. This bed chamber on the second floor is furnished with Gordon family bedroom furniture, including the bed in which Juliette Gordon was born in 1860.

Detail, east elevation. These lions greet visitors to the Andrew Low House.

East elevation, Abercorn Street, overlooking Lafayette Square. In the foreground is the parterre garden, still maintained in the original design.

ANDREW LOW HOUSE

1849, The Colonial Dames of America—Georgia Headquarters
Lafayette Square, 329 Abercorn Street

WHEN JULIETTE MAGILL GORDON married William Mackay Low in December 1886, Willie Low had inherited this house from his father Andrew, who built it for his first wife, Sarah Cecil Hunter Low, nearly forty years earlier. In preparation for the wedding, Daisy Gordon's home, the Wayne-Gordon House, had been remodeled under the direction of Daisy's mother, Mrs. William Washington Gordon. Willie Low also remodeled this house. Both were helped in this work by Detlef Lienau of New York City, who was in Savannah on several projects, including the Telfair Academy. Lienau was retained to prepare the house for the couple's eventual residence, that is for when they might be in Savannah rather than in England.

Lienau added coal grates to the wide marble fireplaces, laid hardwood over the original wide boards on the parlor floor, and installed a bathroom on the second floor. The exterior and much of the interior of the house, however, remained as constructed in 1848 and 1849 for Andrew and Sarah Low. Their architect is believed to have been John S. Norris (1804–1876) of New York City, who first came to Savannah to supervise construction of the granite United States Custom House at Bull and Bay Streets.

John Norris entered the design for that monumental Greek Revival building, the second customhouse in Savannah, in a national competition and won. Norris's biographer, Mary Lane Morrison, described the architect in this way: "An eclectic virtuoso who designed in a blend of many styles" (1980, p. 5). Mrs. Morrison indicated that Norris's contributions to Savannah architecture may exceed those of any other architect who worked in the city during the nineteenth century, including William Jay.

Andrew Low, Willie Low's father and builder of this splendid but classically restrained, early Victorian villa, was one of the most substantial citizens in Savannah and one of the wealthiest men in the British Empire—

Entrance hall details reflected in convex mirror, c. 1825.

Front parlor. The front and rear parlors were furnished and decorated by the Colonial Dames in the late 1970s. The tall windows in the front parlor offer views of Lafayette Square.

Rear parlor. The mid-nineteenth-century American *méridienne* and the crystal chandelier match those in the front parlor.

he remained a British subject with strong ties to England and kept a residence in Liverpool, an important focus of his business. A cotton factor and the leading exporter in Savannah, Andrew left his only son, Willie, a very rich man, who preferred life in London to that in Savannah.

The Lows were Anglo-Americans. In 1853 and 1856, the English novelist William Makepeace Thackeray, lecturing in Savannah, stayed with the Andrew Lows and in a letter home described his host as among the "tremendous men, these cotton merchants." Andrew Low's second wife and Willie Low's mother, Mary Stiles Low, was Thackeray's hostess. Sarah, the first Mrs. Low, died as the house was finished in 1849.

A Scot by birth, Andrew Low had come to Savannah in the 1830s as a young man to join his uncle, for whom he was named, in the firm of A. Low and Company, which he inherited. One of Andrew's partners was Charles Green, also a British subject, whose house, another John Norris design, will follow and complete this cycle of museums.

When Robert E. Lee passed through Savannah in the spring of 1870,

Dining room. This room was furnished by the Colonial Dames in the early 1980s. The fine ironwork of the side verandah can be seen through a tall corner window, beautifully curtained in the style of the 1840s.

Northeast bedroom. This writing desk was used by William Makepeace Thackeray when he was a guest of the Lows in the 1850s.

he stayed with Andrew Low. Mary Stiles Low had died and the house was quiet; Mr. Low was keeping house alone. In 1886, Andrew Low died, bequeathing his fortune and the house to Willie, only months before his wedding to Juliette Gordon. Willie died in 1905, leaving Juliette Gordon Low this house where, during a sojourn in Savannah, she founded the Girl Scouts of the U.S.A., March 12, 1912.

Juliette Low died in this house in 1927, and the next year her heirs sold the property to the National Society of Colonial Dames in the State of Georgia as its headquarters and house museum. (The first president of the Georgia Society of Colonial Dames was Juliette Gordon Low's mother, Mrs. William Washington Gordon II, and Juliette Low was a charter member.)

The house stands on the southwest trust lot of Lafayette Square and Ward, named for the Marquis de Lafayette and laid out in 1837 when Savannah expanded southward into the public lands provided in Oglethorpe's original plan.

South elevation, West Macon Street, on Madison Square. The Green-Meldrim House is the most outstanding Gothic Revival house in Savannah and Georgia, and possibly in the South.

GREEN-MELDRIM HOUSE

1853, Parish House, St. John's Episcopal Church
Madison Square, 14 West Macon Street at Bull Street

HERE IN CHARLES GREEN'S Gothic Revival mansion on Madison Square, one of the outstanding achievements of antebellum Savannah, we reach the finale of a cycle of nineteenth-century houses Savannah values highly enough to preserve as museums and open proudly to the public. We are not the first to reach a conclusion here. In late December 1864, Major General William Tecumseh Sherman ended his March to the Sea through Georgia, staying more than a month as the guest of Mr. Green, a British subject and partner of Andrew Low. As the better part of valor, Savannah had capitulated, thus saving the town, and this house, from the fate Atlanta suffered.

Sherman remembered Charles Green's house and Savannah in his memoirs in this way: "An English gentleman, Mr. Charles Green, came and said that he had a fine house completely furnished . . . and offered it as his headquarters. . . . After riding about the city, and finding his house so spacious, so convenient, with large yard and stabling, I accepted his offer, and occupied that house during our stay in Savannah" (1974, p. 180).

It is well worth quoting General Sherman further for he described the town he had just taken and presented in a telegram to President Lincoln as a "Christmas-gift": "The City of Savannah was an old place and usually accounted a handsome one. Its houses were of brick or frame, with large yards, ornamented with shrubbery and flowers; its streets perfectly regular, crossing each other at right angles; and at many of the intersections were small inclosures in the nature of parks. These streets and parks were lined with the handsomest shade-trees of which I have knowledge, the willow-leaf live oak, evergreens of exquisite beauty; and these certainly entitled Savannah to its reputation as a handsome town more than the houses, which though comfortable, would hardly make a display on Fifth Avenue" (p. 180). Evidently it was difficult for the conquering general to be nice for long: "Would hardly make a display on Fifth Avenue," he said. Perhaps after four years of war, and then occupation by an invading army, this house and others in Savannah had lost some of the luster from the spring of 1861 when William Howard Russell, a war correspondent for the London *Times*, reported: "The wealthier classes have houses of the New York Fifth Ave-

Entrance hall. Many building materials for Charles Green's house were imported from England on his ships, including these ceramic floor tiles.

East elevation. St. John's Episcopal Church towers over the original parterre garden. Tall shutters and windows slide into hidden wall pockets, giving access to the verandah from the double parlors. The ironwork is among the finest in Savannah.

Garden, east elevation.

nue character. One of these, a handsome mansion of rich red sandstone [actually stucco] . . . belonged to my host Charles Green who, coming out of England many years ago, raised himself . . . to the position of one of the first merchants of Savannah" (1943, p.2).

In *Architecture of the Old South, Georgia* (1986), historian Mills Lane describes the Green house more generously than William Sherman, but less so perhaps than William Russell. Lane considers the house to be "the finest surviving Gothic Revival house south of Virginia," and writes: "Green's mansion is a luxurious blend of elaborate design and sumptuous materials, including a massive cast-iron entrance and porches, shutters and windows which slide into hidden wall pockets, oriel windows, English tiles paving the hall and parlor floors and a domed stair with a skylight" (p. 222).

A grandson of Charles Green, the writer and French Academy member Julien Green, came from Paris to Savannah in 1934 and recorded in his diary, published in 1964, some impressions of his grandfather's house. When Julien Green saw the house it was still stuccoed as it had been originally. He described it as a "vast Tudor house, painted a tawny yellow." He said to him it was "both hideous and magnificent" and he characterized the eclecticism of the drawing rooms as "semi-Gothic, semi-Louis XV" but summed up his opinions on a positive note. He thought, "The whole thing remains splendid in a manner that seems peculiar to the Southern states" (1964, p.48).

Opinion will vary about this elaborate house, completed in 1853 according to the design of John S. Norris, of New York City and Savannah. For his client Charles Green, Norris expressed the exuberance and prosperity of the era with an architectural eclecticism that today seems particularly mid-nineteenth century. The house cost $93,000 to construct and was possibly the most expensive house built in antebellum Savannah. When completed, it had just about everything, including indoor plumbing.

Double parlors. A descendent of Charles Green described this elaborate plasterwork as "semi-Gothic, semi-Louis XV."

Charles Green died in 1881, and the house passed to his son, Edward, Julien Green's father. In 1892, Judge Peter Meldrim purchased the property from Edward Green, and it remained in Judge Meldrim's distinguished family until the adjacent St. John's Episcopal Church acquired it for its parish house in 1943.

Facing West Macon Street, now closed to form a new garden between the house and the church, the house enjoys one of the few original parterre garden layouts in Savannah, behind a cast-iron fence on the Bull Street side of the property. Occupying an entire trust lot extending west to Whitaker Street, the house, its gardens, and trees are an integral part of Madison Square, the central square of Jasper Ward, laid out in 1837. Open to the public regularly, the Green-Meldrim House is a National Historic Landmark.

Bull Street at Broughton. This view looks north toward Johnson Square and the City Exchange in 1893, a few years before the arrival of the "horseless carriage." Broughton is the main shopping street of the Savannah Historic District. *Georgia Historical Society.*

West McDonough Street, looking west away from Chippewa Square in 1893. The Moses Eastman House, 1844, 17 West McDonough on the left, is believed to be by the architect Charles B. Cluskey. Today it is the headquarters of the Atlantic Mutual Fire Insurance Company. *Georgia Historical Society.*

The 500 block of East St. Julian Street, looking east toward Washington Square and the Trustees' Garden area. This photograph was taken about 1960, before the restoration of Washington and Warren wards. On the left are two houses, 504 and 510, shown in the following section. *Georgia Historical Society.*

HISTORIC URBAN AND SUBURBAN NEIGHBORHOODS

THE HISTORIC AND PICTURESQUE neighborhoods of Savannah extend from Yamacraw Bluff on the Savannah River, where Oglethorpe first laid out the town, to the Vernon and other tidal rivers on the south, and to the Atlantic on the east. These urban and suburban neighborhoods have developed over time, and some of them have been officially recognized as historic districts. The most widely known historic neighborhood is the old planned city itself, designated a Registered National Historic Landmark in 1966 and often called "*the* historic district" because of its paramount importance. Its listing in the National Register of Historic Places as the Savannah Historic District recognized that primacy.

The boundaries are from East Broad (including Trustees' Garden) to West Broad and from the Savannah River south to Gwinnett Street. (Appendix 2 features maps that describe the city and outlying neighborhoods.) When it was designated a national landmark, the Savannah Historic District was the largest—2.2 square miles—in any major urban area in the United States.

Its architectural and historical integrity was sufficient for registering as a landmark district, yet all had not been perfectly well. Year by year since the turn of the century, the aging but still charming city began to fall into decay. Three of the squares on the western edge of town were cut through for a highway. Row after row of Georgian-style town houses became tenements and great mansions were divided into slum apartments. Hundreds of eighteenth- and early nineteenth-century houses were lost, even some of those by William Jay. Factors' Row and Walk was threatened. "One bright light in all the blight," however, was Mary and Hansell Hillyer's Trustees' Garden rehabilitation project at East Broad Street just after World War II. Their project brought attention to the possibilities of resto-

Gordon Block, 100–129 West Gordon Street. By the 1950s much of the historic district was in this melancholy condition. Today the row is largely restored, and Number 101 is featured in the color section that follows. *Georgia Historical Society.*

ration, and finally in 1955, after the old city market was torn down for a parking garage, a small group of leading citizens rallied and incorporated Historic Savannah Foundation, which at once saved the Isaiah Davenport House on Columbia Square. As a result, thirty years later, old Savannah is actually in better condition than at mid-century, and the Savannah Historic District is nationally recognized as a desirable place to live.

"Historic Savannah" is usually thought of as just the core of the old city, with its unique urban plan and the rich and diverse mixture of private, public, and commercial buildings, but the city contains other areas beyond the boundaries of the landmark district which are also historic and beautiful, and yet are not always seen by visitors.

In 1974, a Savannah Victorian district was listed in the National Register of Historic Places, bounded by Gwinnett Street on the north and Anderson Street on the south, and flanked by East and West Broad streets.

Officially, this Victorian district begins at Gwinnett Street, but, in truth, the southern wards of the Savannah Historic District itself have large concentrations of exceptional Victorian period architecture. Unofficially, Victorian Savannah begins just south of Gaston Street at Forsyth Park, which was created from the City Common in 1851. This park was the culmination of the city as developed according to Oglethorpe's plan of wards-with-squares. And Bull Street, the central spine of the plan, continues visually to the cast iron fountain erected in 1858. The wards that constitute the Savannah Victorian District have no central squares and Forsyth is their "central park."

The designation of the Victorian area of town as a historic district and the leadership of the Savannah Landmark Rehabilitation Project, Inc., has sparked the residents of this late-nineteenth-century suburb into renovat-

Forsyth Park Extension. This turn-of-the-century view looks south toward the monument erected in 1875 "To the Confederate Dead...by the Savannah Memorial Association." Forsyth Park was created from the old City Common south of Gaston Street in 1851, and the park extension was created from the Military Parade Ground in 1866. The entire park now extends from Gaston Street to Park Avenue. *Georgia Historical Society.*

East Taylor Street at Monterey Square, looking east in 1893. The Hugh M. Comer House at 2 East Taylor, on the left, was divided into apartments in the 1930s but reverted to single-family status in the 1970s as the historic district became residentially desirable again. The church on the right was torn down in the 1940s. *Georgia Historical Society.*

Whitaker Street. Trolly car lines can be seen in Whitaker Street in this photograph published in 1893. These lines helped provide access to the Victorian suburbs growing in the southern wards. Today, Whitaker is the main thoroughfare running south on the west side of Forsyth Park. *Georgia Historical Society.*

East Gwinnett at Lincoln Street. On the left is the Queen Anne style masterwork at 223 East Gwinnett, 1891, designed by William Gibbons Preston. This view, published in 1893, looks west toward Forsyth Park Extension; the Confederate monument can be seen in the distance. *Georgia Historical Society.*

Thunderbolt. Thunderbolt is on the west bank of the Wilmington River on the inland waterway southeast of the historic district at Victory Drive. Called Thunderbolt since Indian days—a strike of lightning is said to have brought forth a gushing spring here—it was settled soon after Savannah as a fortified outpost mounted with cannons. It is an incorporated fishing village with shrimp boats docked at picturesque wharves. This view dates from 1893. *Georgia Historical Society.*

Isle of Hope. This view, published in 1893 in *Art Work of Savannah*, looks along Bluff Drive around the bend of the Skidaway River. *Georgia Historical Society.*

Beaulieu, 1893.

ing and restoring their own homes and neighborhood. Leopold Adler II is nationally recognized for his leadership of this project to restore from within by and for the benefit of existing residents. Adler is a Savannah native who also contributed mightily to preservation efforts in the Savannah Historic District.

Further south of the Historic and Victorian districts is the Ardsley Park-Chatham Crescent suburb. In 1984, it too was listed in the National Register. The approximate boundaries are Waters Avenue on the east, Bull Street on the west, Victory Drive on the north, and 54th Street on the south. In the first decades of our century, this neighborhood was developed as two adjacent subdivisions. They are similar in layout to downtown because of the underlying gridiron pattern of streets opened up by landscaped squares and medians. Chatham Crescent has the additional amenity of a Beaux-Arts inspired "City Beautiful" mall, crescent-shaped avenues, and small circular parks. Twentieth-century houses of many styles, types, and sizes are the comfortable and fashionable homes of many Savannahians in this popular garden suburb.

South, southeast, and east of these suburbs are communities on or near the water which have long been popular with Savannahians. Many of the neighborhoods on the salt marsh and tidal rivers and creeks were originally eighteenth- and nineteenth-century plantations and summer retreats. Among them are Thunderbolt, Isle of Hope, Beaulieu, Vernon View, Vernonburg, and White Bluff, and Whitemarsh, Wilmington, and Tybee islands. Tybee Island, also known as Savannah Beach, is at the mouth of the Savannah River and was one of the first places Oglethorpe encountered in 1733 as he began the eighteen-mile river journey up the Savannah to establish a town "to be call'd by that name."

Savannah Beach, on Tybee Island. Tybee, an Indian word meaning salt, is a sea island at the mouth of the Savannah River, approximately eighteen miles by river east of Yamacraw Bluff, where Oglethorpe sited Savannah. Tybee was settled by Oglethorpe in the summer of 1733. First he built a small fort and then, in the spring of 1736, a lighthouse. Savannahians have long coveted summer cottages at Tybee, and area residents in a forty-mile radius would go out—by train until the causeway was completed in 1923—to enjoy the beach or to dance to the big bands at the pavilion. This view of bathers at Tybee—"by the sea, by the beautiful sea"—was made about 1915. *Georgia Historical Society.*

THE HISTORIC DISTRICT

Pulaski Square. In 1837, Pulaski Ward and
Square were laid out and named for General
Casimir Pulaski, who was mortally wounded
in the Siege of Savannah on October 9, 1779.

Apartment-studio, Stoddard's Lower Range, 1858–1859, overlooking the Savannah River.

230 EAST BAY STREET

The waterfront of Savannah, long the center of business activity, is also the site of some of the most important architecture in the city. When cotton ruled the economy of the region, wealthy merchants commissioned the buildings that rise from the water level at River Street to the tall bluff and Bay Street. The designs of architects such as Charles B. Cluskey, John S. Norris, and William Gibbons Preston give the long range of buildings known collectively as Factors' Row a delightfully eclectic appearance, and they have housed a similarly diverse range of tenants.

The apartment-studio of the late Mrs. George (Anna C.) Hunter, for example, was in Stoddard's Lower Range, one of the commercial buildings Norris designed for merchant John Stoddard in the 1850s. Mrs. Hunter, a journalist, preservationist, and sophisticated folk artist, was a principal founder of the Historic Savannah Foundation, Inc., and a long-time resident of the Savannah Historic District.

River Street Plaza, with the river side of
Stoddard's ranges and the Savannah Cotton
Exchange.

South elevation, Bay Street, Factors' Walk entrance, 1818; restored and renovated in 1973. There are three and one-half stories on this side and four and one-half stories facing the river.

206 WEST BAY STREET

This cotton warehouse of ballast stones and brick at the west end of Bay Street is the oldest surviving commercial building on the Savannah River bluff. Built by William Taylor about 1818, it was converted into a modern residence in 1973. The architect for the conversion was Juan C. Bertotto of Savannah, and his clients were a physician and artist, husband and wife, who make this "loft" their home.

Sitting area. This is part of the combination living and dining room on the downstairs level of this dramatic warehouse-to-residence conversion. Below are a studio and two levels still used commercially by shops with River Street entrances.

Bay Street level. A gigantic wooden winch, used to lift freight from ships to the bluff, has been retained as a sculptural element above the stairway. The copper hood and stack for the open fireplace rises next to a large north-facing skylight.

504 AND 510 EAST ST. JULIAN STREET

The preservation and restoration of Washington Ward and Square, which lies between the Trustees' Garden and the business district, was largely accomplished by one family in the 1960s and 1970s. A banker and his wife, Mr. and Mrs. Mills Bee Lane, whose home is in the neighborhood, recognized the potential of this part of the historic district, and through their influence the mix of frame and brick houses, with frame predominating, was renovated and restored. Built from the late eighteenth century through the nineteenth century, together they all relate well in scale and proportion, whatever their materials or ages. Numbers 504 and 510 East St. Julian are cases in point; 504 was built in 1842 for Anne Pitman, and its next door neighbor in 1797 for Charles Oddingsells. Today, these houses proclaim the success of historic preservation in Savannah, which has resulted from cooperation among private citizens and organizations, and tax-supported, governmental agencies.

Dining room and parlor, 504 East St. Julian Street.

South elevations, 504 East St. Julian, 1842, and 510 East St. Julian Street, 1797.

Parlor, 510 East St. Julian Street.

24 HABERSHAM STREET

The John Mongin House was built in 1797 facing the square in Warren Ward. It is one of only one half dozen buildings in Savannah that date from the eighteenth century. This section of town was marked off from the East Common early in the 1790s, part of the first extension eastward of Oglethorpe's town plan. It and adjacent Washington Ward were redeveloped largely through the efforts of Mills Bee and Ann Waring Lane in the 1960s and 1970s. In 1964, the Lanes moved this two-story Federal-style wooden house, only just in time to save it, across the square to this trust lot and had architect John C. LeBey, a Savannah native, put it into its present handsome condition. The current owners have lovingly maintained the house as one of the focal points of this charming neighborhood.

West elevation, 1797; foundation lowered and new porch and doors added in 1960s restoration.

Porch and garden. The back porch looks out over a parterre garden and restored Warren Ward

Parlor. The mantelpiece is from another Savannah house of the same period; the dentil cornice was reproduced from fragments of the original.

503 EAST PRESIDENT STREET

Standing on its original site on the western end of a Greene Square trust lot is this early nineteenth-century, two-story, Federal-style frame house. It stood amazingly well-preserved but sorely neglected until a dentist and his wife, a teacher/musician, purchased it to restore as their home in December 1975. They moved into this proud restoration in the summer of the next year. This house was built in the decade after 1799, when Greene Ward and Square were named for General Nathanael Greene (1742–1786), who settled at Mulberry Grove Plantation near Savannah after the Revolution.

North elevation, built c. 1807; restored 1975–1976.

Parlor. The woodwork, which had survived years of neglect, is original.

Kitchen. This space was adapted during restoration to meet the needs of a modern family.

119 EAST CHARLTON STREET

The Battersby-Hartridge House was built in 1852 for William Battersby, an English citizen and Savannah cotton merchant who was associated with Andrew Low. The designer is unknown but could have been John S. Norris, a New Yorker who practiced in Savannah and designed the neighboring Andrew Low House. The house faces the Low House front garden and Lafayette Square, the centerpiece of Lafayette Ward, which was created in 1837 and named for Marquis de Lafayette (1757–1834). Battersby and his wife, Sarah Hartridge of Savannah, lived in the house until after the Civil War. They created the walled garden, one of a few surviving antebellum parterre gardens and the only one that is viewed from a side entrance porch in the Barbadian or Charleston style. After the Battersbys moved to England to live, the house became the residence of Julian Hartridge, Susan Battersby's brother and great-grandfather of the present owner.

Walled garden. One of the few surviving original garden plans in Savannah.

North elevation, East Charlton Street, 1852; interior modifications in the late 1880s by William Gibbons Preston, the Boston architect.

Parlor. The tall windows of this spacious sitting room look out on one of the "outdoor living rooms" of Savannah, Lafayette Square. The house is designed to relate to the square.

East elevation, Barnard Street, 1845; restored and renovated in 1972.

Parlor. In Savannah, "parlor floors" are one story above the street. They are called the first floor even though they are not at street level. The ceiling medallion and the mantelpiece in the Greek Revival style are both original to the house.

321 BARNARD STREET

In 1845, Bernard Constantine, a merchant, built this two-story frame house on the northwest trust lot facing Pulaski Square. In the early 1970s, after years of neglect, Constantine's house was restored and renovated by its present owner, a historian/publisher. On a raised basement, the parlor floor reached from a flight of steps, it is typical of Savannah houses of the 1840s and 1850s. The side porch, based on the design of the original front porch, was added during renovation and allows a pleasant view of Pulaski Ward and Square and the walled garden of grass and boxwood.

Bedroom, second floor.

Side porch. The owner has said: "The porch is designed to reproduce the details of the original front porch and the spirit of nineteenth-century Savannah. An afternoon visitor, iced tea or mint julep in hand, can overlook the green garden and a panorama of old houses in the neighborhood."

South elevation, Jones Street, 1861; restored and renovated in 1975.

22 EAST JONES STREET

Tree-shaded Jones, divided east and west by Bull, is one of the most appealing residential streets in the historic district. From end to end, it is lined with nineteenth-century houses, some detached, some paired, and some attached as rows. Many of them are built of the local brick called Savannah grey, as is this four-story detached house. Built in 1861, just before the Civil War, its style seems ten or twenty years earlier. When the present owners acquired the property in 1975, the three floors above the English basement had been practically gutted. Admiring the spaciousness this promised, they retained Savannah architect Juan C. Bertotto to help them mold the space to an advantage. The dramatic results admirably demonstrate the freedom-loving taste of our day, interpreted with a sense of restraint that respects the classic Savannah, Georgia, Georgian exterior.

Double parlors. The owners collect the works of local artists and the trees of Jones Street seen through the tall parlor windows seem reflected in the batik over the arched marble mantelpiece.

Dining room. This two-story room on the garden side captures the sense of space opening out and up that the owners sought in their renovation. They commissioned Ivan Bailey, Georgia iron-master, to fashion this modern chandelier.

South elevation, East Jones Street, 1860;
renovated by several owners, the last in the
mid-1980s.

Garden. A walled garden laid out with respect
for Savannah precedents, but rather more
spacious than any other in the historic district.

204 EAST JONES STREET

This house was built for Abraham Minis II, a grandson of the first Abraham Minis, who came to Georgia in July 1733. Since completed in 1860, it has faced serenely south on East Jones Street in Lafayette Ward, seemingly possessed with the inner peace that great beauty sometimes imparts. A symmetrical, stately, and sophisticated villa, part Greek and part Italianate, it has had many admiring owners since it was built. It was designed by an architect well known in his day, Stephen Decatur Button (1813–1897) of Philadelphia, a classicist whose Alabama State Capitol (1847) in Montgomery may also be cited for excellence. The present owners purchased the property in 1984 and did not occupy the house until eighteen months of meticulous work had readied it for their superb furnishings.

Double parlors. The parlors, divided by sliding pocket doors, retain their original woodwork and mid-nineteenth-century mantelpieces; above the mantels in each parlor hang identical mirrors with exceptional gold frames featuring naturalistic carvings of animals and birds.

Library. Above the mantelpiece is Brigadier
General Archibald Campbell Douglas Dick,
1886, by John Singer Sargent (1856–1925), the
most celebrated portrait artist of his day.

Dining room. Above the sideboard in this room of baronial proportions is a portrait of the wife of the brigadier general in the library, also by Sargent. Above the Georgian console table on the left is a work by the American impressionist Frank W. Benson of Mary Sullivan, c. 1900.

222 EAST JONES STREET

Built in 1857 as speculative housing, this classic Savannah grey brick town-house was purchased in 1973 and has been lovingly restored over a period of years as the home of a youthful museum consultant. The Savannah Historic District has been brought to life since the 1950s by such courageous, talented people attracted by the culture and historic charm of Savannah. By 1973, it had been divided into four rather squalid apartments, and the new owner personally has transformed the entire property inside and outside, including a side garden that was a "dirt yard" when he began his restoration. Even in its run down condition, the many original features that had survived attracted him to begin this long labor of love.

South elevation, East Jones Street, 1857; restored and renovated since 1974. Among the owner's gifts to passersby is the exterior iron-work executed for him by Ivan Bailey, the Georgia iron-master. The hand rails for the porch steps feature native, low-country flora and fauna, and a functional boot scraper. It is among the most noteworthy ironwork from any period within the historic district.

Garden. This walled garden has a south-north and an east-west axis. It evolved from a swept dirt yard into this green oasis in the style of the nineteenth-century gardens of Savannah.

Parlor. Above a sofa that descended in his family is a portrait of the owner's great-grandfather by Elliot Daingerfield.

326 BULL STREET

The Eliza Jewett House stands on the northeast trust lot of Madison Square across from the Green-Meldrim House. It was built in 1843 as the home of a well-to-do woman who owned rental property; the brick row behind her home was Jewett's. In the mid-1950s, one of the early leaders of the preservation of the Savannah Historic District, Alida Harper Fowlkes, bought and renovated the house, converting it into rental units. In 1975, the present owners reconverted the house into their own residence. Of brick covered with stucco, this four-story house is a good example of the dignified, classical houses that lined the streets of antebellum Savannah. The interior architecture is far more elegant than the restrained exterior indicates.

Parlors. The mid-nineteenth-century classicism of these adjoining parlors could not be more redolent of Georgian period England. The rear parlor has been set up as a dining room.

West elevation, Bull Street, overlooking Madison Square, 1843; renovated 1950s, restored 1975.

Entrance hall. In Savannah the main staircase was often set apart from the foyer by a screen of classical columns. Framed in the doorway is a view of Madison Square, as though it were the "front yard" of this house, an illusion shared by other houses around the squares of historic Savannah.

East elevation, Bull Street, overlooking
Monterey Square, 1860–1871, restored 1960s.

Stairhall. The floor of English ceramic tile is
similar to that in the Green-Meldrim House,
also designed by John Norris. This stair
ascends to a domed skylight, a feature much
used by Norris.

429 BULL STREET

John S. Norris, an accomplished architect from New York who built many fine buildings in Savannah, designed this mansion for General Hugh W. Mercer in 1860 just as the Civil War began, and it was not completed until several years after the war. The picturesque and romantic eclecticism of taste during that era is exemplified by this large house facing Monterey Square. Abandoned in the 1960s, it was restored and furnished in the late 1960s and early 1970s by a Savannah dealer in antiques and fine arts, who had long played an important role in the preservation of the Savannah Historic District. With its rear garden and carriage house, it occupies the entire northeast trust lot of Monterey Square.

Front parlor. This large room looks out on Monterey Square and is furnished in a style reminiscent of the English country house as it has been interpreted in the last quarter of the twentieth century.

101

Study. The wide expanses of window in this corner room take full advantage of the fine views of the neighborhood and provide excellent ventilation.

Dining room. Furnished with late-classical antiques, c. 1830, this room overlooks the rear garden and shows again how "light and airy" this big house was designed to be—the outdoors are embraced throughout by wide windows tall enough to step through onto verandahs and balconies.

Center parlor. A spacious, open, yet disciplined plan is a symphony of classical geometry, with arches repeated as though themes in a musical composition.

South elevation, East Taylor Street, 1860; restoration in progress. The rosy beige of the weathered stucco is vintage Savannah, classic Savannah *par excellence*.

128 EAST TAYLOR STREET

Calhoun Ward and Square were laid off and named in 1851 for the Honorable John C. Calhoun (1782–1850) of South Carolina. Only a few years later Mary E. Demere built this house as her home on Taylor Street facing the square. Using the most enlightened restoration techniques developed by preservationists, the current owner, a dealer in fine antiques and art, is carefully restoring the interior and furnishing it with decorative arts of the antebellum period, c. 1820–1860.

Entrance hall. This is the owner's design laboratory as he restores the house room by room. The painted floorcloth was executed by Robert Christian, a Savannah artist specializing in *faux* finishes.

Gordon Block.

Garden. A long verandah, which serves the parlor floors of both 101 and 103 West Gordon, is part of the walled garden. The crape myrtle tree in the right foreground is believed to be nearly as old as the house.

101 WEST GORDON STREET
GORDON BLOCK

In the decade before the Civil War, handsome rows of houses were built; the longest row of all was four-story Gordon Block, 101–129 West Gordon Street, from Whitaker west to Barnard Street, in Chatham Ward. In the 1920s, when the family of the owner of 101 West Gordon moved into the house at the eastern end of the row, this part of Savannah was no longer considered fashionable, or even quite respectable. It was a daring move for the parents of the current owner, but sixty years later he is still at the same address and has also purchased the next house, 103, part of which he occupies while renting the rest. In 1959, he moved out for a year so a total restoration could be undertaken, including installation of central heat. He and members of his family have indeed been pioneers of the preservation of the Savannah Historic District.

Parlor. Reflected in the large pier glass over the mantelpiece is a sitting room dressed in light summer loose covers. The *faux marbre* mantel decoration was renewed in 1959 by the late Christopher Murphy, Jr. (1902-1973); Murphy was a talented artist whose drawings, etchings, and watercolors of Savannah are much sought. To the left of the mirror, above a Virginia walnut side table that belonged to the owner's mother, is a Chris Murphy watercolor of Thunderbolt, the fishing village east of town.

North elevation, West Gordon Street, 1853;
restored and renovated c. 1927 and 1959. The
ironwork of Gordon Block is considered among
the finest in Savannah.

2 EAST TAYLOR STREET

The exteriors of houses built in Savannah after the Civil War remained very much in character with their earlier neighborhoods. This four-story Italianate house, built in 1880 for Hugh M. Comer, president of the Central of Georgia Railroad, is a post-war example of the traditional Savannah house on a high basement, the parlor floor reached by a flight of steps. The interior, however, is another matter. A better example of fashionable taste in the 1880s, both in America and in England, could not be found. The elaborate black chimneypiece with mirrored over-mantel exemplifies the Aesthetic Movement in interior decoration and points to major changes in taste that were underway. The house remained in the Comer family until 1936, when it was sold and divided into apartments. In 1978, the present owners bought the property and began their long-term restoration.

Parlor. By 1880, the Aesthetic Movement in the arts was a well-established fact; the chimney-piece of the Comer House shows it had come to Savannah. As with many other Savannah houses, large windows overlook a side garden and a central square that seems to be an extension of the home.

South elevation, East Taylor Street, overlooking Monterey Square, 1880; restored and renovated 1978.

Parlor. The plan of the interior was recast to create a new stairway and this combination sitting and dining area on the garden side. The oak fireplace wall and the oak doors and over doors were designed as modern statements of traditional architecture by Atlanta architect Eugene Surber, a specialist in historic preservation.

510 EAST STATE STREET
ANDERSON ROW

The persistence of classical English traditions in the buildings of Savannah and the benefits of historic preservation are well represented by this house. In style and type this row of Savannah grey brick houses might have been built before the Civil War but is dated 1890. On March 10, 1890, this notice appeared in the *Savannah Morning News*, "Mr. Randolph Anderson is building six handsome two-story brick houses on State at Price." The architectural survey Historic Savannah Foundation conducted in the 1960s rated Mr. Anderson's row "excellent," and the foundation purchased it to protect it from further deterioration. Number 510 was an unrenovated shell in 1969 when the owner, an Atlantan, bought it as a restoration project and second home. With a definite spark of creativity and the help of several consultants, including two architects, the Atlantan transformed her "tenement" into such a cozy townhouse that she began in 1973 to reside here all year.

South elevation, East State Street, 1890; restored and renovated 1969-1971. Anderson Row faces south in Greene Ward west of Greene Square.

26 EAST GASTON STREET

Gaston Street is on the southern edge of Monterey Ward and of the area developed according to Oglethorpe's original town plan of wards with central squares. In the southeast corner of the ward, on two sixty feet by ninety feet lots facing Forsyth Park, stands the Mills Bee Lane House. It was designed in 1909 by Mowbray and Uffinger of New York. This firm began to design Savannah buildings in 1907 when it was asked by Mr. Lane to design his bank on Johnson Square. With a foreground of live oaks festooned with Spanish moss and a background of church spires, Justin Uffinger's crisp red brick Georgian Revival seems very much at home in Savannah. The house has remained in the same family since it was completed in 1910.

South elevation, Gaston Street, overlooking Forsyth Park, 1910.

Parlor. The fireplace wall of the green parlor continues the Georgian Revival style of the exterior quite happily into the interior. In the overmantel hangs a portrait of Mrs. Mills Bee Lane by the American portrait artist Hilda Belcher.

Detail of sitting room. This fine classical revival chimneypiece was rescued from an in-town early nineteenth-century house when it was about to be demolished in the 1920s. Above it hangs a portrait by Hilda Belcher of the present owner's grandmother.

Forsyth Park, Forsyth Ward. The area defined by Gaston Street on the north, Drayton and Whitaker streets on the east and west, and Hall Street on the south was laid out in 1851 and named for Governor John Forsyth (1780–1841). The original park was designed by William Bischoff, a Bavarian landscape gardner, and an elaborate cast iron fountain was commissioned for the center of the park in 1858. It was manufactured by James Beebe Company of New York and was based on a fountain exhibited at the Crystal Palace in London in 1851. The park was expanded as the Forsyth Park Extension was designated a Military Parade Ground in 1866.

SOUTH OF GASTON

South elevation, West Hall Street, 1888.

118 WEST HALL STREET

Near the southern limits of the Savannah Historic District and just west of Forsyth Park is a picturesque house in the Victorian Queen Anne style that might be at home in Bedford Park, a garden suburb of London. This house was designed by Alfred S. Eichberg, an architect who was born in New York in 1859 and came to Atlanta in 1882, then to Savannah in 1886. He built the house for J. P. Williams in 1888. It is one of the best expressions in Savannah of the Arts and Crafts, or Aesthetic Movement, a phenomenon that originated in England in the 1860s and became fashionable in America in the 1870s and 1880s. The domestic architecture of this movement is called Queen Anne, a romantic asymmetrical style in which the front elevation expresses the informality of the interior plan and suggests early English architecture with an eclectic assortment of half-timbering, towers, turrets, gables, bays, and small-paned and stained glass windows. The plan is open with rooms of different shapes and sizes, merging into one another, usually opening off of a large entrance hall from which an intricate paneled staircase ascends.

Entrance hall. Typical of the Queen Anne style house was an elaborate fireplace in a large, wainscoted stairhall that was also the main entrance to the house. Through the hall two small studies are visible. Eclectic collections fill these rooms, and interesting accoutrements abound; they reflect a love of craftsmanship and design and an eye for fascinating detail—and they fit perfectly in this house.

Dining room. Ornate mirrored overmantels
and tiled fireplaces such as those shown here
were features of the Queen Anne interior. The
delicate sculpted and painted plasterwork is
found in varying patterns throughout the
ground floor.

Parlor. Bay and oriel windows and stained or colored glass panels were important characteristics of this picturesque style. The flamboyant overmantels with carved and turned wood trim are a celebration of the influence of "modern" machinery on nineteenth-century architecture.

Library. This polygonal room is equipped with records, books, and comfortable English club chairs from the nineteenth century. The stained glass window is original to the house.

225 EAST HALL STREET

A talented architect from Boston was responsible for designing many important Savannah buildings, including this house near the southern boundary of the Savannah Historic District. William Gibbons Preston, F.A.I.A. (1842–1910) helped to transform the face of Victorian Savannah with twenty-three commissions for buildings of various types. This transformation reflected the post-Reconstruction prosperity of Savannah, based on cotton, naval stores, lumber, and phosphates. Preston's major residential design for the city was this house built as the home of George Johnson Baldwin in 1887 and now restored. George Baldwin was an unusually successful businessman whose fortune was founded on phosphates. His lengthy obituary March 5, 1927, described this house as "the center of social and cultural life" in Savannah. The present owner had been looking for a late-Georgian style row house, but George Baldwin's red-brick Queen Anne style villa won out. The house is again a center of social and cultural life, as it had been during the tenure of the man who had it built.

Stained glass panel in library.

North elevation, East Hall Street, 1887.

Detail of terra cotta ornament from chimney on east elevation. The Queen Anne style called for red brick with molded terra cotta details, which often appeared on tall, highly ornamented chimneys.

Stairway. In overall form and intricate detail it has every characteristic of the Queen Anne style. The rich dark staircase and colored glass panels contrasting with large clear panes is typical, as is the window seat in the bay.

Reception room. Just inside the entrance foyer, opening off of the main stairhall, is this small formal receiving room for visitors who might not be proceeding further into the house.

Entrance hall. A major feature of the Queen Anne style was a central stairhall, sometimes called a living hall. Other major rooms opened into this impressive space. W. G. Preston's interior ornamentation is a romantic interpretation of early English Renaissance.

701 WHITAKER STREET

This two-story frame Queen Anne style house faces east toward the southern end of Forsyth Park where Forsyth Park Extension begins. Built in 1897 for Joseph B. Chestnutt, a naval stores factor and dealer, it takes full advantage of a corner site on Whitaker Street, a main north-south thoroughfare through the Savannah Historic District. Floor length windows with stained glass transoms open out onto generous verandahs that reach out toward the park with twin copper-roofed turret porches. A second story porch on the West Hall side also looks out onto the park for a glimpse of green and a breath of air. The open plan of the interior, with suites of connecting rooms, also seems designed for the needs of a Savannah summer. Carved and turned woodwork and ornate fireplaces with colorful patterned tilework all speak of the disciplined but picturesque richness of detail and craftsmanship that is the hallmark of the Queen Anne style—here represented by one of the most appealing examples in the Victorian wards south of Gaston.

East elevation, Whitaker Street, overlooking Forsyth Park, 1897; restored and renovated in 1970s.

Entrance hall. Through the front door and across the verandah are the moss-draped live oaks of Forsyth Park.

HISTORIC SUBURBS

Victory Drive. Flanking a procession of hundreds of tall palm trees planted in honor of the United States victory in World War I, the four lanes of Victory Drive extend east from the Ogeechee Road to Thunderbolt. This landscaped parkway, which symbolically separates downtown Savannah from its southern suburbs, passes through the northern edge of the Ardsley Park-Chatham Crescent neighborhood and is lined with large early twentieth-century homes.

Washington Avenue. Oak-shaded Washington Avenue runs east and west parallel to and several blocks south of Victory Drive through the middle of the Ardsley Park-Chatham Crescent neighborhood. This rural area was developed as adjacent subdivisions in the first decades of the twentieth century, when the advent of the automobile made the "commute" to downtown Savannah feasible, and the modern houses set among landscaped squares and crescent-shaped avenues made suburban living fashionable. The Ardsley Park-Chatham Crescent suburb, now listed as a historic district, dates from 1910.

Number 39 Washington Avenue. This Ardsley Park home was built in 1910 for Harry Hays Lattimore (1874-1931), one of the principal partners of the Ardsley Park Land Corporation. The mansion-scaled, neoclassical revival "model home" for the subdivision was designed by Percy Sugdin, the Savannah city engineer. It became the residence of H. H. Lattimore's son Ralston and his family in the 1950s. Double parlors, featuring screens of fluted Ionic columns, are glimpsed from the large entrance stairhall. The house is decorated with the late Ralston Lattimore's collection of Christmas originals, including his annual Christmas globes, handmade by him according to yearly themes, such as "Garden of Peace," shown here at the foot of the stairs.

2 Pierpont Circle, Gordonston. Gordonston is a garden suburb east of the historic district and north of Victory Drive. It was built just before World War I by William Washington Gordon III, Juliette Gordon Low's brother. The "model home" at 2 Pierpont Circle was built in 1917 by Savannah architect and builder Olaf Otto. The design is based directly on the Wayne-Gordon House, the Gordon family home on Oglethorpe Avenue. Otto used the measured drawings of that house, now the Juliette Gordon Low Center, made by Detlef Lienau in 1886. A Gordonston nomination to the National Register of Historic Places has been submitted.

Bluff Drive, Isle of Hope. Although much of the Isle of Hope was plantation land belonging to such notable early colonists as Noble Jones, this quiet residential area grew from a nineteenth-century summer resort village on the west bank of the Skidaway River. Isle of Hope remains one of the most charming of the historic tidewater suburbs of Savannah. On the right is a raised, classical cottage at 3 Bluff Drive built in 1848 by Major John B. Gallie.

TIDEWATER SUBURBS

The Habersham-Rockwell House, c. 1840,
Vernonburg.

VERNONBURG
AND BEAULIEU

Vernonburg and Beaulieu are
nearly due south of the Savannah Historic District. Vernonburg is out White Bluff Road
on the west bank of the Vernon River, and Beaulieu is on
the east bank off Whitefield
Avenue. The Habersham-Rockwell House, circa 1840, faces
east on a beautiful moss-
draped tract of land that has
been called "Bonnie Doon"

Colonel Charles H. Olmstead's home at
Beaulieu on the east bank of the Vernon River,
from Olmstead's *Art Work of Savannah*, 1893.

View of Vernonburg in 1893, from the Vernon River south of the "township."

since the 1870s. Vernonburg and Beaulieu, both settled since the mid-eighteenth century, are suburban neighborhoods where many Savannahians now have their homes. Beaulieu was the site of William Stephen's plantation. Vernonburg has been a small community separate from Savannah since 1742 and a chartered "township" since 1866. It has a mayor and a strong sense of landed, riverside privacy. In 1984, the population of Vernonburg was 178.

James Oglethorpe, Robert Castell, and Paul Fourdrinier: English Palladianism, the Founding of Georgia, and the Savannah Town Plan

"Under George II Palladianism conquered . . . the high places of architecture—the great patrons, the government offices—[and] through the medium of books and prints the whole of the vernacular."

John Summerson, *Georgian London*, 1945.

DURING THE REIGNS OF GEORGE I AND II, there was a widespread revival of interest in the architecture and town planning of the first renaissance classicist in England, Inigo Jones (1573–1651), and in the work of Jones's mentor, the sixteenth-century Italian master Andrea Palladio (1518–1580), author of an unusually influential treatise, *The Four Books of Architecture*. The revivalists, led by Lord Burlington, are called English Palladians. They published a series of books almost as influential as Palladio's—in one of them Inigo Jones is called "Vitruvius Britannicus." Robert Castell and Paul Fourdrinier were part of this Burlingtonian circle of Georgian period Neo-Palladians, and James Oglethorpe was well acquainted with their work.

Palladian classicism was part of the "intellectual baggage" of the gentlemen of Georgian England. An avid reader of ancient history, Oglethorpe subscribed to two of the most important publications of the Burlingtonian school of renaissance architectural theory. Both had large plates engraved by the master London engraver Paul Fourdrinier, the engraver to the English Palladians who several years later engraved The Trustees' View of Savannah "as it stood the 29th of March 1734." Oglethorpe is listed among the subscribers to William Kent's *Designs of Inigo Jones* (1727) and Robert Castell's privately printed *Villas of the Ancients Illustrated* (1728).

The residential squares of Oglethorpe's Savannah, as of those in the West End of London, were ultimately derived from Inigo Jones's early seventeenth-century design of Covent Garden Piazza, the first house-lined square in London. And Jones derived his inspiration from Palladio's *Four Books*; in an early English translation of Palladio in chapter 16 of the third book, entitled "Of the Piazze, and of the edifaces that are made around them," Palladio wrote: "It is necessary that in cities . . . there should be piazze . . . ample places to walk, to discourse, and bargain in; they also afford a great ornament. . . . In sea-port towns they must be near the port" (1971, p. 72).

Dedicated "To the Right Honourable Richard Earl of Burlington,"

To the Honble the Trustees for establishing the Colony of Georgia in America This View of the Town of Savanah is humbly dedicated by their Honours Obliged and most Obedient Servant Peter Gordon

Robert Castell's *Villas of the Ancients Illustrated* was the first attempt to reconstruct ancient Roman villas and their surrounding estates from classical descriptions. Castell was interested in classical concepts of landscape architecture and town planning and said: "Vitruvius had the same Rules for situating Villas as he laid down concerning Cities," mentioning the need for "good Roads," "navigable Rivers," "fertile Land," "wholesome Water," and "healthy Air" (1728, p. 18).

During the year after Robert Castell published his *Villas of the Ancients*, Castell died of small pox, a victim of the horrible conditions in the notorious Fleet Prison where he was incarcerated for debts—quite possibly for those incurred in publishing his treatise. At his death, Castell was engaged in an English translation of *Vitruvius*, the ancient Roman source of classical architectural theory and practice. Castell's needless death in debtor's prison became a cause célèbre, a determining factor in Oglethorpe's interest in prison reform and in the creation of a utopian colony and town in America. In *Landmark Homes of Georgia, 1733–1983*, I wrote: "Some scholars have considered Castell's folio to be the direct source for the design of Savannah. Indirect is perhaps a better word. Castell's text and engravings are characteristic of the way English architectural humanists thought about locating an appropriate site for a large estate and then distributing the elements in a regular fashion" (Mitchell 1982, p. 17).

James Oglethorpe's association with Robert Castell and with the work of Paul Fourdrinier, the master engraver of the English Palladian school who later engraved an elegant prospect view of the appearance of Savannah in 1734, sheds light on the world in which Oglethorpe and the other Georgia Trustees founded Savannah. The series of six house-lined residential squares, or wards,—with their special layout of streets, varied building sites, and lanes that constituted Savannah in 1743 when Oglethorpe left Georgia permanently—was his interpretation of English renaissance town planning transferred and adapted to the special needs of the southernmost English colonial capital.

As it had throughout George II's realm, English Palladianism found its way to Georgia by means of the influence of books and prints on talented people such as James Oglethorpe, a gentleman well acquainted with the best thinking of his era on how to design an ideal town that would be new and, at the same time, classic—which it continues to be.

1. The Stairs going up.
2. Mr. Oglethorpe's Tent.
3. The Crane & Bell.
4. The Tabernacle & Court House.
5. The publick Mill.
6. The House for Strangers.
7. The publick Oven.
8. The draw Well.
9. The Lott for the Church.
10. The publick Stores.
11. The Fort.
12. The Parsonage House.
13. The Pallisadoes.
14. The Guard House and Battery of Cannon.
15. Hutchinson's Island

APPENDIX TWO

Notes on the Map

Historic Downtown Savannah is divided east and west by Bull Street. House numbers increase heading east or west away from Bull Street.

Traffic around the squares can be tricky for the newcomer or tourist, as downtown Savannahians can attest. When entering the square, the driver must yield the right-of-way. While in the square, the driver has the right-of-way.

There are some one-way streets to facilitate the flow of traffic to and from downtown Savannah. These streets are indicated on the map with yellow arrows. Some streets, like Montgomery, Lincoln, and East Broad, are one-way to a certain point and then become two-way.

The white arrows preceding highway names on the map indicate that the driver should proceed in that direction for more specific signage information.

Map Key

1. John Rousakis Plaza
2. Cotton Exchange
3. City Hall
4. Emmett Park
5. Factors' Walk
6. Trustees' Garden
7. William Scarbrough House
8. Franklin Square
9. Ellis Square
10. Johnson Square
11. Reynolds Square
12. Warren Square
13. Washington Square
14. County Courthouse
15. Liberty Square
16. Telfair Academy of Arts and Sciences
17. Telfair Square
18. Wright Square
19. Oglethorpe Square
20. Owens-Thomas Museum
21. Columbia Square
22. Isaiah Davenport House
23. Greene Square
24. Juliette Gordon Low Birthplace and Center
25. Savannah Visitors' Center
26. Elbert Square
27. Civic Center
28. Orleans Square
29. Chippewa Square
30. Colonial Park Cemetary
31. Crawford Square
32. Pulaski Square
33. Green-Meldrim House
34. Madison Square
35. Andrew Low House
36. Lafayette Square
37. Troup Square

Map Legend

- ■ Historic Sites and Museum Houses
- ■ Squares
- ■ National Historic Landmark District
- ■ Victorian Historic District

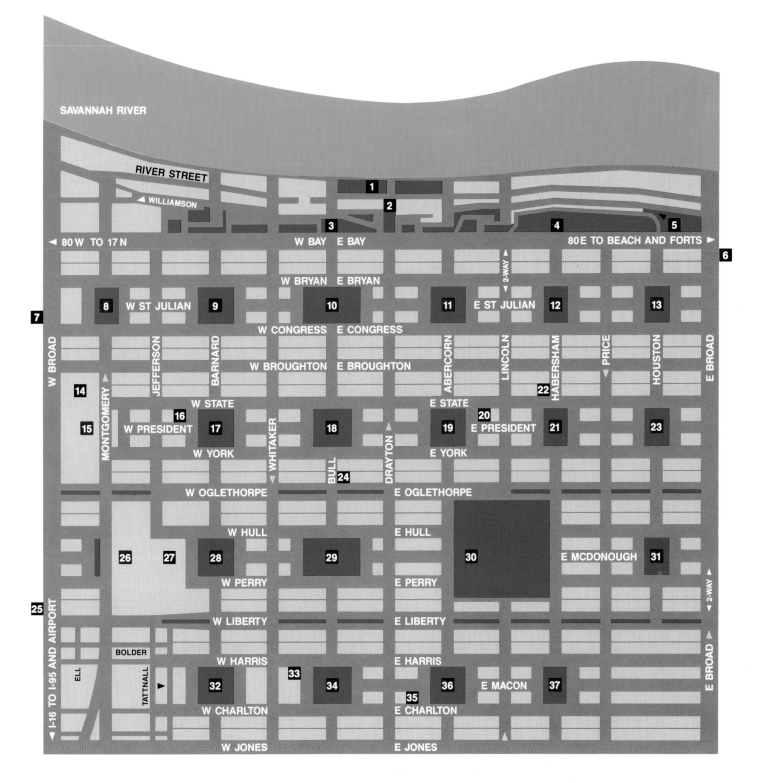

38. Chatham Square
39. Monterey Square
40. Calhoun Square
41. Whitefield Square
42. Forsyth Park

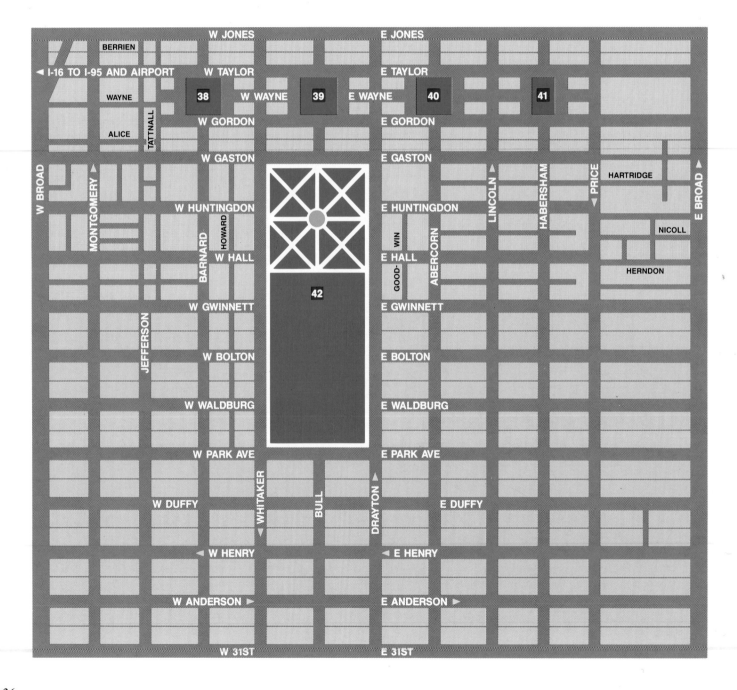

Historic Savannah Neighborhoods

Map Legend

■ Historic Neighborhoods

▬ Interstate Route

▬ U.S. Route

● State Route

Map Key

1. Historic Downtown Savannah
2. Ardsley Park, Chatham Crescent, and Victory Drive
3. Gordonston
4. Thunderbolt
5. Vernonburg
6. Isle of Hope and Bluff Drive
7. Tybee Island and Butler Avenue
8. Coffee Bluff
9. Beaulieu

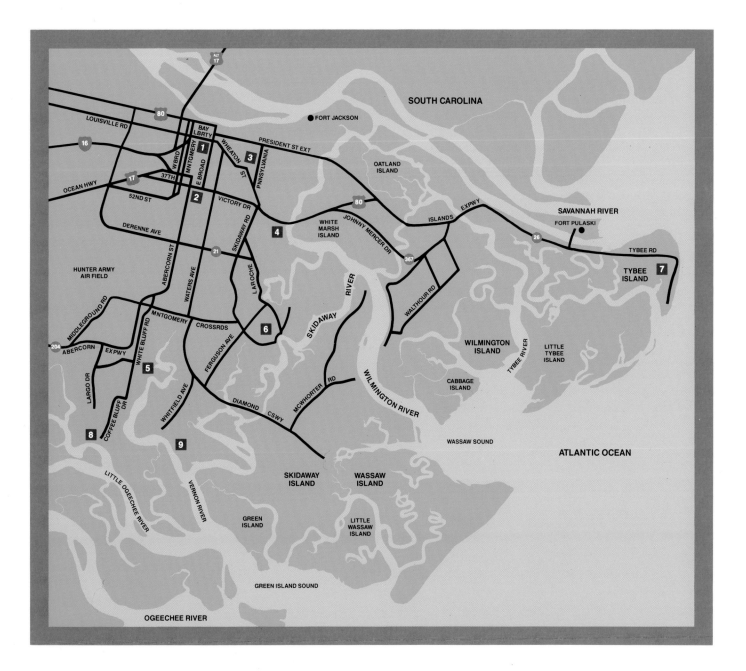

SOURCES

Savannah itself was the primary source—houses, buildings, squares, neighborhoods, and topography.

Unpublished Materials

Author's Collection. Atlanta, Georgia. "Custom House—Savannah, Letter from the Secretary of the Treasury." 27th Con., 2d sess., 1842. H. Doc. 138. "William Jay, contract for the erection of . . . a custom-house . . . destroyed by . . . extensive conflagration in the year 1820."

Gamble, Thomas. *The Romance of William Jay, Savannah Architect of 1818-1825*. Thomas Gamble Collection, Savannah Public Library, 1945.

Matero, Frank G., and Zachary N. Studenroth. *Owens-Thomas House: Historic Structures Report*. Savannah: Telfair Academy, 1984.

McDonough, James Vernon. "William Jay: Regency Architect in Georgia and South Carolina." Ph.D. diss., Princeton University, 1950.

The Georgia Historical Society. Savannah, Georgia. Photographic archive of Savannah subjects; original copy of Oglethorpe-Gordon-Fourdrinier View, 1734; Cerveau painting, 1837; the Walter C. Hartridge Ms. Collection.

Stembridge, James Wesley. "The Settlement of Georgia: Town Planning and Architecture in the Colonial Period." Master's thesis, Georgia State University, 1971.

National Archives. Washington, D.C. General Records of the Treasury Department, R.G. 56 Letter dated May 20, 1817 from Archibald S. Bulloch to William H. Crawford regarding "a suitable site for the custom-house."

_____. Records of General Accounting Office, R.G. 217, No. 44488. Auditor's report, August 9, 1822, and other pages associated with the erection of a customhouse in Savannah, including articles of agreement with William Jay dated May 27, 1819.

Published Materials—Books

A Child's View of Savannah's Squares. Savannah-Chatham County Board of Education, 1981.

Bacon, Edmund N. *Design of Cities*. New York: Viking Press, 1967.

Bell, Malcolm, Jr. *Savannah*. Savannah: Historic Savannah Foundation, 1977.

_____. *Savannah Ahoy!* Savannah: Pigeonhole Press, 1962.

Binney, Marcus. *Sir Robert Taylor*. London: George Allen and Unwin, 1984.

Bragg, Lillian Chaplin. *Old Savannah Ironwork*. Savannah: Pigeonhole Press, 1957.

Buckingham, James Silk. "The Slave States of America." In *The Rambler in Georgia*. Edited by Mills Lane. Savannah: Beehive Press, 1973.

Castell, Robert. *Villas of the Ancients Illustrated*. London, 1728. (Engravings by Paul Fourdrinier.)

Colvin, Howard. *Biographical Dictionary of British Architects*. London, 1978.

Crane, Edward A., and E. E. Soderholtz. *Examples of Colonial Architecture in Charleston, S.C. and Savannah, Ga*. Boston: Boston Architectural Club, 1895.

Cruickshank, Dan, and Peter Wyld. *London: The Art of Georgian Building*. London: Architectural Press, 1975.

Davis, Harold E. "Social and Cultural Life in Colonial Georgia." In *The Fledgling Province*. Chapel Hill: University of North Carolina Press, 1976.

DeBolt, Margaret Wayt. *Savannah: A Historical Portrait*. Virginia Beach: Donning Co., 1976.

Egmont, Earl of. "The Journal of the Earl of Egmont." In *Abstract of the Trustees Proceedings, 1732-38*. Edited by Robert G. McPherson. Athens: University of Georgia Press, 1962.

Fancher, Betsy. *Savannah: A Renaissance of the Heart*. Garden City, N.Y.: Doubleday, 1976.

Girouard, Mark. *Cities and People*. New Haven: Yale University Press, 1985.

Glazier, Capt. Willard. *Peculiarities of American Cities*. Philadelphia, 1886.

Gordon, Peter. "The Journal of Peter Gordon." In *Our First Visit in America: Early Reports from the Colony of Georgia*. Edited by Trevor R. Reese. Savannah: Beehive Press, 1974.

Green, Julien. *Diary 1928-1957*. Edited by Kurt Wolff. New York: Harcourt, Brace, and World Inc., 1964.

Harden, William. *A History of Savannah and South Georgia*. Atlanta: Cherokee Publishing Co., 1967.

_____. *Recollections of a Long and Satisfactory Life*. Savannah: Review Printing Co., 1934.

Harris, John. *The Artist and the Country House: View Painting in Britain*. London: Sotheby Parke Bernet, 1979.

Hartridge, Walter Charlton. *The Green-Meldrim House*. Savannah: Society for the Preservation of Savannah Landmarks, 1943.

Hartridge, Walter Charlton, ed. *The Letters of Robert Mackay to His Wife, 1795-1816*. Athens: University of Georgia Press, 1949.

Hartridge, Walter Charlton, and Christopher Murphy, Jr. *Savannah*. Columbia, S.C.: Bostick and Thornley, 1947.

Historic Preservation Plan for the Central Area. Savannah, 1968.

Historic Savannah. 2d ed. Savannah: Historic Savannah Foundation, 1979.

Horton, Corinne Ruth Stocker. "Savannah and Parts of the Far South." Part 12 of *The Georgian Period*. New York, 1902.

Hyde, Ralph. *Gilded Scenes and Shining Prospects*. New Haven: Yale University Press, 1985.

In Savannah Perspective. Savannah: Historic Savannah Foundation, 1980.

Jackson, Harvey H. and Phinizy Spalding, eds. *Forty Years of Diversity: Essays on Colonial Georgia*. Athens: University of Georgia Press, 1984.

Jones, Charles C., Jr. *History of Savannah*. Syracuse, N.Y.: D. Merson and Co., 1890.

Kennedy, Roger G. *Architecture, Men, Women, and Money in America*. New York: Random House, 1985.

Lane, Mills. *Architecture of the Old South: Georgia*. Savannah: Beehive Press, 1986.

_____. *Savannah Revisited: A Pictorial History*. 3d ed. Savannah: Beehive Press, 1977.

Lane, Mills, ed. *General Oglethorpe's Georgia: Colonial Letters, 1733-1743*. 2 vols. Savannah: Beehive Press, 1975.

_____. *The Rambler in Georgia*. Savannah: Beehive Press, 1973.

Lerski, Hanna. *William Jay, 1792-1837*. Lanham, Md.: University Press of America, 1983.

Lee, F. D., and J. L. Agnew. *Historical Record of the City of Savannah*. Savannah: J. H. Estill, 1869.

McPherson, Robert G., ed. *The Journal of the Earl of Egmont, 1732-1738*. Athens: University of Georgia Press, 1962.

Mackay, Charles. *Life and Liberty in America; or, Sketches of a Tour . . .in 1857-8*. London: Longmans, Green and Longmans, 1859.

Martin, Van Jones. *At Home in Savannah: Great Interiors*. Savannah: Golden Coast Publishing Co., 1978.

Mitchell, William R., Jr., and Van Jones Martin. *Landmark Homes of Georgia, 1733-1983*. Savannah: Golden Coast Publishing Co., 1982.

Moore, John Hammond, ed. "A View of the South, 1865-1871." In *The Juhl Letters to the Charleston Courier*. Athens: University of Georgia Press, 1974.

Montgomery, Sir Robert. *A Discourse Concerning the Designed Establishment of a New Colony to the South of Carolina*. London, 1717.

Morrison, Mary Lane. *John S. Norris: Architect in Savannah, 1846-1860*. Savannah: Beehive Press, 1980.

Oglethorpe, James Edward. In *General Oglethorpe's Georgia: Colonial Letters, 1733-1743*. Edited by Mills Lane. 2 vols. Savannah: Beehive Press, 1975.

Olmstead, Charles Hart. *Art Work of Savannah*. Chicago: W. H. Parish Publishing Co., 1893.

Olsen, Donald J. "The Eighteenth and Nineteenth Centuries." In *The Town Planning in London*. New Haven: Yale University Press, 1964.

Palladio, Andrea. 1738. *The Four Books of Architecture*. New York: Dover Publications, 1971. Facsimile.

Plumb, J. H. "America and England, 1720-1820: the Fusion of Cultures." In *American Art, 1750-1800: Towards Independence*. New Haven: Yale University Art Gallery, 1976.

Rauers, Betty, et al. *Sojourn in Savannah*. Rev. ed. Savannah: Printcraft Press, 1984.

Rasmussen, Steen E. *London: The Unique City*. Rev. ed. Cambridge: Massachusetts Institute of Technology Press, 1983.

Resse, Trevor R., ed. *Our First Visit in America: Early Reports from the Colony of Georgia*. Savannah: Beehive Press, 1974.

Reps, John W. *Town Planning in Frontier America*. Princeton: Princeton University Press, 1969.

Russell, William Howard. *London Times*. In *The Green-Meldrim House*. By Walter Charlton Hartridge. Savannah: Society for the Preservation of Savannah Landmarks, 1943.

Savannah Victorian District Design Guidelines. Savannah, 1980.

Sherman, William T. *"War Is Hell!"*. Edited by Mills Lane. Savannah: Beehive Press, 1974.

Sholes, Albert E., comp. *Chronological History of Savannah*. Savannah: Morning News Print, 1900.

Sieg, Chan. *The Squares: An Introduction to Savannah*. Norfolk, Va.: Donning Co., 1984.

Spalding, Phinizy. *Oglethorpe in America*. Chicago: University of Chicago Press, 1977.

Summerson, John. *Georgian London*. London: Pleiades Books, 1945.

Tailfer, Patrick. "A True and Historical Narrative of the Colony of Georgia in America, 1741." In *The Clamorous Malcontents*. Savannah: Beehive Press, 1973.

Thackeray, William Makepeace. *A Collection of Letters of Thackeray, 1847–1855*. New York: Charles Scribner's Sons, 1887.

Theus, Charleton M. *Savannah Furniture*. Savannah: Georgia Historical Society, 1973.

Voss, Frederick S. *John Frazee, 1790–1852, Sculptor*. Washington City and Boston: The National Portrait Gallery, the Smithsonian Institute, and the Boston Atheneum, 1986.

Waring, Joseph Frederick. *Cerveau's Savannah*. Savannah: Georgia Historical Society, 1973.

Wilson, Adelaide. *Historic and Picturesque Savannah*. Boston: Boston Photogravure Co., 1889.

Wittkower, Rudolf. *Palladio and English Palladianism*. New York: Thames and Hudson, 1983.

Wood, Louisa Farrand, et al. *Behind Those Garden Walls in Historic Savannah*. Savannah: Historic Savannah Foundation, 1982.

Articles

Adler, Leopold, II, et al. "The Savannah Story." *Historic Preservation*. 21 (January-March 1969): 6-21.

Bassett, Beth. "The Antiques of Savannah." *Brown's Guide to Georgia*. 7 (January 1979): 43f.

Bell, Laura Palmer. "The Vanishing Gardens of Savannah." *Georgia Historical Quarterly*. XXVIII (September 1944): 196-208.

——————. "A New Theory on the Plan of Savannah." *Georgia Historical Quarterly*. XLVIII (June 1964): 147-165.

Cornforth, John. "The Green City of Savannah." *Country Life*. 157 (January 16, 1975): 142-145.

——————. "A City of Spacious Vistas." *Country Life*. 157 (January 30, 1975): 270-272.

——————. "New Life for a Southern City." *Country Life*. 157 (February 2, 1975): 334.

Coulter, E. Merton. "The Great Savannah Fire of 1820." *Georgia Historical Quarterly*. XXIII (March 1939): 1-27.

Hopkins, Emma B. "Regency." *Interior Design and Decoration*. 12 (April 1939): 46f.

Hopkins, Emma B., and Nancy McClelland. "American Federal and Empire." *Interior Decorator*. 98 (April 1939): 21f.

Hunter, Anna C., ed. "Special Historic Issue." *Savannah Magazine*. 2 (February 1971): 1-40.

Jones, George F. "Peter Gordon's (?) Plan of Savannah." *Georgia Historical Quarterly*. LXX (Spring 1986): 87-101.

Kennedy, J. Robie, Jr. "Examples of Georgian and Greek Revival Work in the Far South." *Architectural Record*. (March 1907).

Kirk, Russell. "House on Reynolds Square." *National Review*. 24 (February 18, 1972).

Lane, Mills. "Living with Antiques: The Bernard Constantine House in Savannah." *Antiques*. 111 (June 1977): 1210-1213.

Lee, Clermont H. "The Squares of Savannah." *Planning and Civic Comment*. 17 (March 1951): 24.

Lerski, Hanna. "The Scarbrough House." *Society of Architectural Historians Journal*. 33 (October 1974): 227.

Mackay, Charles. "Transatlantic Sketches, Savannah and the Sea Islands." *Illustrated London News*. (July 3, 1858).

Matlock, Carol. "Savannah." *American Preservation*. 2 (February-March 1979): 9-24.

Mitchell, William Robert, Jr. "A Savannah Landmark, The Richardson-Owens-Thomas House." *Southern Accents*. 8 (January-February 1985): 48-61.

Morrison, Mary Lane. "On Savannah Squares." *Nineteenth Century*. 2 (Spring 1976): 6-13.

Muldawer, P. "Criteria of Urban Design Relatedness." *Historic Preservation*. 23 (January 1971): 29-35.

Osman, M. E. "Savannah's Victorian District." *American Institute of Architects Journal*. 67 (February 1978): 50-55.

Stevenson, Frederic R. "Charleston and Savannah." *Society of Architectural Historians Journal*. 10 (October 1951): 5-9.

Williams, Roger M. "Savannah." *Saturday Review*. 3 (August 21, 1976): 16-18.

Winchester, Alice, ed. "Antiques at Savannah." *Antiques*. 91 (March 1967).

Zimmerman, Helena. "Savannah." *Architectural Digest*. 33 (September-October 1976): 126-131.

Colophon Sources

Boorstin, Daniel J. *The Americans: The Colonial Experience*. New York: Vintage Books, 1958, p. 325.

Meggs, Philip B. *A History of Graphic Design*. New York: Van Nostrand Reinhold, 1983, p. 140.

INDEX

Index to Architects, Builders, Artists, and Craftsmen
(The Table of Contents is the index to houses illustrated.)

A Note on the Type

The text of this book was set in Caslon 540, with the display type *Classic Savannah* set in Caslon Shaded. William Caslon (1692–1766) was a young English engraver in 1720 when he first tried his hand at type design. His success was immediate and widespread, and from the 1720s until the end of the eighteenth century virtually all English printing used Caslon fonts. Printer Benjamin Franklin (1706–1790) introduced Caslon to colonial America in the 1740s, where it was also used extensively. Caslon's type designs were probably used in Savannah after the arrival of the first printing press in Georgia in 1762. Georgia was the last of the thirteen colonies to acquire, through government subsidy, a printing press. There were already about forty presses operating throughout the colonies at that time.

William Caslon's type styles owe their popularity, then and now, to a straightforward practicality, sturdiness of form, and eminent legibility.